PUERTO RICAN COOKBOOK

PUERTO RICAN
COOKBOOK

BY

ELIZA B. K. DOOLEY

ILLUSTRATIONS BY
THE AUTHOR

COACHWHIP PUBLICATIONS
Greenville, Ohio

Puerto Rican Cookbook, by Eliza B. K. Dooley
© 2018 Coachwhip Publications

Published 1948.
No claims made on public domain material.

CoachwhipBooks.com

ISBN 1-61646-449-6
ISBN-13 978-1-61646-449-3

For Mary

In Memory of Isabel

DEDICATION

ISABEL

"Thy name was writ in water—it shall stand:
And tears like mine will keep thy memory green,
As Isabella did her Basil-tree."—The Grave of Keats.

No book of my recipes could ever be compiled without a dedication to Isabel, for anything connected with cookery is inevitably associated with her memory.

When I came a bride to a new and strange country Isabel was my guide and helper. "Yes, Missis, I reckon we can buffle on." And "buffle on" we did.

Born in St. Christophers, (St. Kitts) she came to Puerto Rico a small child; the pride of birth was in her veins and she always referred to herself as a "British object." The whites of her eyes and her strong white teeth shone smilingly out of her velvety black face. Clad in light percales, enveloped in a full starched apron, her delight in dress and color found its vent in the care and attention she gave her head handkerchiefs. These she collected from other islands and took the greatest joy in them; red and yellow, blue and green plaids with occasionally a plain color to vary; they were of madras a yard square, and folded diagonally the long side was put about her head, brought around in front and tied with the folds neatly disposed, the ends tucked in. Wearing a very bright one from Martinique she laughingly left the ends of a perky bow standing upright in imitation of the way they do it in the French islands. Frequent washings gave them a softness of color although they really never faded. A black and white check was reserved for funerals and for Holy Week. At night she wore a fine, plain white linen one, for even at night her head was not uncovered. We would scarcely have known her without her turban for she was never without it, it seemed to be the badge that represented her love and gift for service.

Then life went on at a more leisurely tempo, there was time for gracious and harmonious living. Those were the days of open house— the doors indeed, were never closed, there was always provision for an extra guest or two.

We cooked on a great old stove of Spanish tiles, using charcoal for fuel. A pickaninny was always around to fan the flame which burned with steady, bright heat. Nothing quite approaches a charcoal fire. To this day old housekeepers who have yielded to modern kitchens and have gas stoves, still keep an "anafre", a brazier to cook steaks, chops, and the inevitable red beans of the kitchen; the full flavor of the food is brought out by the steady cooking. I recall when gas was installed Isabel refused to part with the old stove. "But, Isabel, I should think you would like a new gas stove." "No, mistress, I'se prepared to meet my Jesus, but I ain't prepared to meet Him ahead of time"! So she went along with the old-fashioned equipment.

I early gave up the idea of making innovations. Once having been given a breadmixer, she gazed fascinated as it stirred the sponge. "Knowledge is increasin'!" was her comment. But a few weeks later her strong right hand was mixing the sponge. A rosebush was planted in the mixer.

She took such a pride in the house, in the cooking and in all she did, that the veriest drudgery took on a holiness and became a beautiful thing by the love she put in the merest detail. In her humble way she truly found the art of living.

Everything went by rule of thumb. One night there was unusually good cake, light and delicious. When asked for the recipe, "Well you creams de butter." "How much?" "Oh, jes' enough to mix up." "But can't you tell me the amount?" "Well dat depen's on de size of your cake."

"But Isabel, success depends on accuracy." "Oh, go 'long chile, dis cake depen's on me an not you. You take yourself out de kitchen." "But you measure accurately, don't you, Isabel?" "Yes, yes, Missis, deedy I does, measurements is measurements and accuracy is accuracy. I don't say but I puts a lil' more or a lil' less now an den, but it always comes out and dats de answer. I don' need no prescriptions."

"You know, Isabel, that at cooking school the first lesson is care of the ice-box and sink." (This with a suggestive look at the sink.) "Oh, you go 'long, Missis, don' you go none dem lessons, you know too much 'bout dat already."

It was true she needed no "prescriptions" for she never had to ask what to put in a dish, but by some sixth culinary sense or subtle reckoning concocted delectable food.

For years she waited for a baby in the house. "On dat day I come out de kitchen." And true to her word, when Mary did arrive, the first face I saw as the steamer pulled into the dock, was the smiling one of Isabel. She took the wee one into her arms, I found a new cook installed in the kitchen, and from that time to the day of her death Isabel trailed her beloved Mary.

When the baby could scarcely talk her religious training began.

Seated on the edge of the bed, drilling in prayers; "Say it, 'Hallowed be Thy name.' " "I won't." "Say it!" "I won't, my name's Dooley!"

Coming from Sunday School, bursting with pride; "Harwood Hull, great big boy, couldn't say de Creed; Charles Colmore, great big boy, de Bishop's son, couldn't say de Creed; lil' Mary Dooley, only six years old was de only child in Sunday School could say de Creed—Oh God, I hope she may live!" Accompanying the family to church, she knelt on the marble floor; kneeling benches and cushions were for white folks—not for humility.

Mary came from kindergarten with a folded paper frame they had made for George Washington's picture on the event of his birthday. Distressed to find George was no more: "But mother, if he is dead why do we keep his birthday?" Explanations followed and immediately Isabel rose to the occasion. "Why, me heartstrings, Judge Washin'ton was one of de foremostest Judges of New Nited States!" After a visit to Mount Vernon, a few years later, Mary showed Isabel her collection of pictures, among them the tomb. Greatly intrigued, Isabel discovered a second sarcophagus in the picture. "Who is de oder coffin?" "Well, that's Mrs. Martha Washington." Consternation: "Oh, goodness, Mistress, you don' mean to tell me pore Mis' Washin'ton's *dead too!*"

History and geography were extremely hazy in her mind. The World War was in some dim way caused by the revolution in Santo Domingo. Her patriotism ran high. Every stray cockroach within reach of her slipper was vindictively slatted as "one less German!" Curiously enough, the flying cockroaches of these islands are of the genus "germanicus", had she known it!

For more than twenty-eight years Isabel reigned in my kitchen. We came to think of her as a town institution, she found servants for my friends, she comforted their children. Others of my friends have their Isabels, not only in the art of cookery but in the art of faithful service; Amanda, Augusta, Catherine, Louise, remain of the old days and of the old school but their steps are faltering, their ranks are thinning.

I never see tamarinds but I think of old Fanny; aged, worn-out, half blind, she was pensioned off and spent her days visiting around. When tamarind season came she was sure to appear. "Missis, jes' a few tamarinds and ole Fanny goin' make you some syrup." "Very well, Fanny, help yourself." A bagful gathered, "Now Missis, jes some sugar to go with and Fanny make you syrup." The syrup made, of course I bought it. Once on her way she lost a dollar bill from her apron pocket and came bawling and lamenting. The cook said, "Don' bawl, de Missis is out, she ain' hearin' you." But having some emergency money she was given a dollar. The next time I saw her I sympathized with her loss. "Yes Missis. I did feels bad but I cried at ten houses and got ten dollars."

Tricky? yes, they tricked us and harassed us and bothered us, but that was no comparison with the gift for loyalty which they possessed and the affection they showered upon us.

A new comer hearing of Isabel thought her a prize worth having and came to consult her, offering a great increase of wages. Her rebuff was so complete that she had to tell of it herself. Isabel listened to all her offers, gazing off into space. Then she looked at her sternly: "You know, lady, dey is jes' one pusson goin' separate me from my mistress, an' dat's de *Lord God Almighty.*"

And so it was. When in her last illness she felt her strength waning she begged to be carried up into the house from her outside room. So she was carried into Mary's room, put to bed in Mary's bed and went to meet her Maker with Mary's name on her lips.

Isabel has gone; she was to some just an old black woman, but with her we buried something finer than pearls in a crown, than the stars in their courses; a devotion not one of us merited, a belief in our superior wisdom, an affection never to be equaled; a love that, as nearly as we may experience on this earth, approached the divine. We shall not see her like again.

CONTENTS

A PUERTO RICAN COOKBOOK

HOME

From "Seven Sonnets on Puerto Rico"
GRACE SPENCER PHILLIPS

The Great Creator carves His wonders old
Upon Celestial Spheres. We search each land
With puny mind to learn the meaning told
In His Great Plan. There grew at His command
Lands great and small, all cast in different mold;
Vast seas alike were fashioned by His hand.
We cannot grasp His marvels grand and bold,
But little lands we all can understand.

This Isle, a sonnet in its form and grace,
Offers a place of rest and peace secure;
On every plain and verdant slope, we trace
A lovéd garden made in miniature.
Some deep, divine decree of mercy's shown
To every man that calls this land his own.

INTRODUCTION

WHEN one looks over the Puerto Rican landscape, one sees flame-tree, orange-tree, bougainvillea vine, pineapple, banana, and sugar-cane. One sees in the towns the stone houses and superb old yellow fortifications of the Spanish, modern office buildings and a familiar pattern in white marble. These things are Puerto Rico, yet none of them is Puerto Rican. The small Caribbean island, seemingly so withdrawn from outside contacts has, during four centuries, gathered in gifts from all corners of the globe and made them her own. The Spaniards brought the orange here from Spain, the banana from Africa, the pineapple from the South Seas, and the sugar-cane from India. Mexico gave the bougainvillea, Asia the flametree. Even the now ubiquitous hibiscus is a foreigner who decided to stay. Even the lovely nameless primrose-flowering weed that at some seasons overruns all the banks and open plots in San Juan is an immigrant, whose seeds were brought in years since in the wrappings of a freight vessel and at once exuberantly made the city their own.

Under and amid all this imported richness and fecundity are those indigenous things which persist: the unique violet tree, of which barely forty full-grown specimens are left in the world; the fragrant white orchid that grows on the summit of El Yunque; wild plantain, wild eggplant, rose-apple and custard-apple, and the Puerto Rican "cherry."

Mrs. Dooley's cookbook, then, is truly representative of Puerto Rico not merely because of the native Puerto Rican dishes which she gives us an opportunity to savor, but because of the many dishes which she has set down that are suitable to the Puerto Rican table and welcomed there, yet cooked after recipes from far distant regions.

The United States and Europe, and especially the sister islands of the West Indies—British Jamaica and Barbados, French Martinique, Dutch Curaçao, St. Thomas of Danish days—have contributed to the feast which she spreads for us. But all these recipes have enjoyed a sea-change; all have become Puerto Rican, written in terms of what one can buy in the market-place in San Juan or Ponce; written so explicitly that not even an inexperienced cook will be afraid to attempt the new dish, and so alluringly that the seasoned housewife can read these pages with the deep whole-hearted satisfaction of a musician reading a score.

Mrs. Dooley was blessed by Nature with the hospitality and tact of the true hostess; she was blessed by circumstance with that pearl of cooks to whose memory she so lovingly dedicates this volume. And out of the garnered wisdom of a quarter-century during which "dinner with the Dooleys" meant, in Puerto Rico, sparkling wit and gracious companionship, perfect service, and food and wine to be remembered as an experience—with a Henry W. Dooley cocktail, in all probability, inaugurating the evening—Mrs. Dooley has set down for the public benefit this enticing and satisfying anthology of delights.

—MUNA LEE.

PLANTS FOR PUERTO RICO

"That our sons may be as plants grown up in their youth."
—*Psalms* 144: 12.

COLUMBUS discovered Puerto Rico on his second voyage, landing on November 19, 1493. This voyage was not only one of discovery but of colonization; he brought seeds of the Seville orange, lemons and sugar-cane for the new islands, as well as vegetables, horses, cattle and goats.

With Columbus on this second voyage was Ponce de León who returned from Santo Domingo to the island in 1508 and became the first governor. His wife, Doña Inés, was the first white woman, and their three children the first white children in Puerto Rico so that they established the first Christian home. Two clearings were made for planting, trying out the cultivation of the many seeds and plants brought with them. One of them is still visible and the locale goes by the name of *Los Reyes Católicos* (The Catholic Kings) named by Ponce de León for their majesties. Doña Inés planted her garden, watching its growth and teaching her Indian women new ways of cookery, so strange to them, and experimenting with produce of the country, so new to her.

They found many root crops in the little farms of the Indian natives: the "cassava", the "yautía", the "maní" (peanut) and maize. The pleasant lanes were shaded by many fruit trees growing wild; the

"anon", the "guanabana", the "guava", the "caimito" and the "mamey".
Native pineapples were planted in the hedges. From the deep sea and
the running streams was obtained an abundance of fish.

Coconut palms, breadfruit, the mango and the sugarcane were
brought in later by the Spaniards. It is said the Spanish sovereigns
gave orders that no ship should sail to the western hemisphere without
taking plants, seeds and animals to begin agricultural pursuits in the
new world. Not only did Spain bring plants and seeds from the
mother country, but with customary enterprise the Spaniard carefully
nurtured a great variety of American foods and shipped them across
the ocean to Europe, thence to other parts of the world. The Americas
were richer in variety of foodstuffs than all the rest of the world.
Before the close of the 16th Century, turkeys, Indian corn, cassava,
tobacco, potatoes, chocolate and many fruits had been taken to Europe
in commerce.

Restricted though it has been geographically, many contacts have
combined to make Puerto Rican cooking what it is; the vegetables and
fruits of the country cooked in the simplest fashion by the aborigines
were the food of the early Spaniards; then Portuguese, who came in as
soldiers, brought additional ways of using them; negroes imported
from Africa as slaves must have known some of the tropical plants
and ways of using them; Italian settlers brought their own distinctive
ways of cooking; as time went on the neighboring islands, Dutch,
English, French and Danish, influenced the native cookery. For 157
days Puerto Rico was a British possession.

During colonial times commerce developed with the northern continent and the sailing ships brought down produce from the north in
exchange for local articles of food; with the advent of steamships,
modern refrigeration, palatial steamers and now airplane service, it is
hard to believe that once we had no northern apples or even took
Danish butter out of a can! In northern markets we now find besides
citrus fruits, the mangoes, avocados and indeed most of our native
fruits in season.

It would be impossible to give adequate credit to the sources of
these recipes. They have been gathered together over a period of forty
years' housekeeping in Puerto Rico. Popenoe's *Manual of Tropical
Plants, Economic Plants of Puerto Rico* by Cook & Collins, Grosourdy's
Medical Botany helped to identify many products botanically. The
actual recipes have been collected from housewifely friends, from
government bulletins, from the Home Economics Department, Univer-
sity of Puerto Rico, and from neighboring islands. Those of northern
kitchens have been modified to substitute things grown in this island.

Mostly, they are from the hand of Isabel. It is said that Americans are, as a rule, loath to depart from old habits of eating, because we are not entirely free from sectional prejudice, perhaps, but there is no doubt that exploring the use of native products gives one a more varied and interesting diet. Those who seem to have learned early the secret of maintaining the best of their traditions by adapting themselves to and utilizing the resources of the country, keep their health in the tropics and sub-tropics. If this collection benefits a newcomer, feeling new to the country and new to housekeeping under strange conditions, as I did myself, I shall be rewarded for the labor of compiling it.

—ELIZA B. K. DOOLEY.

COCKTAILS

"It's the snap and the go of the thing."

A COCKTAIL is an appetizer and should differ from other drinks in that it contains bitters. Originally cocktails were made from gin, whiskey or brandy, and by adding vermouth they became a more blended drink. A dry cocktail is one in which little, if any, sugar is used. A sweet cocktail is an anachronism; it defeats its purpose.

The main idea a manufacturer of liquor has, is to keep the liquor smooth. If ice has rough edges it bruises the liquor and destroys its smoothness. Therefore, if ice is broken into pieces and then has warm water poured over it the sharp edges are taken off and the molecules of the liquor are not shattered. The result will be a smooth cocktail, as it should be. The making of a good cocktail is an art and a ceremony, with every detail followed with care. Haphazard methods and combinations result in very indifferent cocktails, to say the least.

Cocktails are not "native" to Puerto Rico but many have become native through use of local mixes. Those "imported" have been so long with us that we claim them as legitimate as our neighbors in "the States."

Have plenty of space in the containers; chill the container and glasses too; put bitters in first, and liquors of greater density next; stir a cocktail slowly and stir in one direction. If you shake it, shake it slowly. Enough ice should be used so that the melting of the ice adds one-third to the volume. Cocktails should be made at the last moment and not be permitted to stand. A cherry or an olive may be placed in the glass but each guest should be asked his preference. As a rule the cherry accompanies a sweet drink and the olive a dry one; Angostura Bitters may be used, or Boker's; orange bitters are used in conjunction with others. Avoid too many bitters and do not have cocktails too strong.

A mixing-glass holds 12 ounces, 6 jiggers, or 24 tablespoonfuls. A pony holds one ounce or 2 tablespoonfuls.

APPLE BRANDY COCKTAIL

Bitters   Lemon peel
Apple brandy

A mixing-glass half-full of fine ice, two dashes Peyschaud or Boker's bitters, one jigger apple brandy. Mix and strain into a cocktail-glass. Add a piece of twisted lemon peel.

ARMOUR COCKTAIL

Bitters   Italian vermouth
Sherry   Orange peel

Fine ice in mixing-glass, three dashes orange bitters, half a jigger sherry, half a jigger Italian vermouth. Mix, strain into cocktail-glass. Add a piece of orange peel.

BRANDY COCKTAIL

Syrup   Brandy
Bitters   Lemon peel

A mixing-glass half-full fine ice, two dashes gum-syrup, two dashes Peyschaud or Boker's bitters, one jigger brandy. Mix and strain into cocktail glass. Add a piece of twisted lemon peel.

BRANDY COCKTAIL—OLD-FASHIONED

Sugar   Lemon peel
Bitters   Brandy

Crush lump of sugar in a whiskey-glass with sufficient hot water to cover the sugar, add one lump ice, two dashes bitters, a small piece lemon peel, one jigger brandy. Stir with a small bar-spoon. Serve leaving spoon in the glass.

BRANDY COCKTAIL—FANCY

Maraschino   Lemon
Bitters   Sugar
Brandy

Fix a mixing-glass half-full of fine ice, add three dashes maraschino, two dashes Peyschaud or Boker's bitters, one jigger brandy, one dash orange bitters; mix. Strain into cocktail-glass, the rim of which has been moistened with a piece of lemon dipped in powdered sugar.

BRANT COCKTAIL

Bitters   Brandy
Creme de Menthe   Lemon peel

Mixing-glass half-full fine ice, two dashes Angostura Bitters, one-third of a jigger white creme de menthe, two-thirds of a jigger of brandy. Mix well. Strain into cocktail-glass; twist a piece of lemon peel over the top.

BROWN COCKTAIL

Bitters   French vermouth
Holland gin   Lemon peel

Fill a mixing-glass half-full of fine ice, add three dashes Boker's bitters, one-half jigger Holland gin, one-half jigger French vermouth; shake until cold. Strain into cocktail-glass; twist a small piece of lemon on top.

CALISAYA COCKTAIL

Calisaya   Whiskey   Lemon peel

Half a jigger calisaya, half a jigger whiskey, one small piece lemon peel, half a mixing-glass full fine ice. Mix well, strain into a cocktail-glass.

CHAMPAGNE COCKTAIL

Sugar   Lemon peel
Bitters   Champagne

Put into a long thin glass one lump cut-loaf sugar saturated with Boker's bitters, and one lump of ice, a fair sized piece of lemon peel; fill the glass three-fourths full with cold champagne. Stir with a spoon and serve.

CHAMPAGNE COCKTAIL—FANCY

Sugar   Lemon
Bitters   Champagne

Into a long thin glass, put two lumps of sugar; wet one of the lumps with Peyschaud bitters. Add three lumps of ice and the rind of a lemon. Catch one end of the lemon rind on the edge of the glass. Fill the glass nearly full with cold champagne. Stir with a bar-spoon and serve.

CHOCOLATE COCKTAIL

Egg   Port wine
Bitters   Sugar

Break a fresh egg into a mixing-glass half full of fine ice, add one dash bitters, one jigger port wine, one teaspoonful fine sugar. Shake well and strain into a cocktail-glass.

CIDER COCKTAIL

Sugar   Lemon peel
Bitters   Cider

Saturate a lump of cut-loaf sugar with Boker's bitters. Place it, with one lump of ice and a small piece of lemon peel, in a thin cider-glass, then fill up with cold cider. Stir with spoon and serve.

COFFEE COCKTAIL

Sugar   Brandy
Egg   Nutmeg
Port wine

Fill a mixing-glass half-full of fine ice; add one teaspoonful powdered white sugar, one fresh egg, one pony port wine, one pony of brandy. Shake thoroughly and strain into a large cocktail-glass. Grate a little nutmeg on top before serving. Strange to say it has a taste somewhat like coffee, hence the title.

COUNTRY COCKTAIL

Bitters   Whiskey   Lemon peel

Put into a mixing-glass half-full of fine ice, two dashes of orange bitters, two dashes Boker's bitters, one piece lemon peel, one jigger rye whiskey (no sweetening). Mix and strain into a cocktail-glass.

GIN COCKTAIL—HOLLAND

Bitters   Holland gin
Syrup   Lemon peel

Take a mixing-glass half-full of fine ice, two dashes Boker's or Peyschaud bitters, two dashes gum-syrup, one jigger Holland gin. Mix; strain into a cocktail glass. Add a piece of twisted lemon peel.

GIN COCKTAIL—OLD-FASHIONED HOLLAND

Sugar   Lemon peel
Bitters   Holland gin

Put a lump of sugar in a whiskey-glass; add enough hot water to cover the sugar. Crush the sugar; add a lump of ice, two dashes Boker's bitters, small piece of lemon peel, one jigger of Holland gin. Mix with small bar-spoon and serve with spoon in glass.

GIN COCKTAIL—PLYMOUTH

Bitters   Plymouth gin   Lemon peel

Mixing-glass half-full fine ice, three dashes orange or Peyschaud bitters, one jigger Plymouth gin. Mix well, strain into cocktail-glass. Add a small piece lemon peel.

GIN COCKTAIL—TOM

Bitters   Tom gin   Lemon peel

Have mixing-glass half-full of fine ice; add two dashes Peyschaud or Boker's bitters, one jigger Tom gin. Mix well, strain into cocktail-glass and add a small piece of lemon peel.

GIN COCKTAIL—OLD-FASHIONED TOM

Sugar   Lemon peel
Bitters   Tom gin

Mix same as Old-Fashioned Holland Gin Cocktail, using old Tom gin in place of Holland.

HARVARD COCKTAIL

(Brought to Puerto Rico by Harvard "grads.")

Syrup   Brandy
Bitters   Seltzer
Italian vermouth

Mixing-glass half-full of fine ice; one dash gum-syrup, three dashes Boker's bitters, half a jigger Italian vermouth, half a jigger of brandy. Mix and strain into a cocktail-glass, then fill up with seltzer and serve quickly.

IRISH COCKTAIL

Bitters   Acid phosphate
Whiskey   Italian vermouth

Mixing-glass half-full of fine ice, three dashes orange bitters, two dashes Horsford's acid phosphate, one-half jigger whiskey, one-half jigger Italian vermouth. Mix well, strain into cocktail-glass.

JERSEY COCKTAIL

Sugar   Lemon peel
Bitters   Cider

Put one lump of ice in a thin cider-glass. Add one-half tablespoonful of fine sugar, two dashes Boker's bitters, one piece lemon peel. Fill up with cold cider. Stir well, and drink while effervescent.

LIBERAL COCKTAIL

Syrup   Whiskey
Bitters   Lemon peel

Fill a mixing-glass half-full fine ice, add one dash syrup, half a jigger Picon bitters, half a jigger whiskey. Mix, strain into cocktail-glass. Add a small piece of lemon peel on top.

MANHATTAN COCKTAIL

Syrup   Whiskey
Bitters   Lemon peel
Italian vermouth

Fill a mixing-glass half-full of fine ice, add two dashes gum-syrup, two dashes Boker's bitters, one-half jigger Italian vermouth, one-half jigger whiskey. Mix, strain into cocktail-glass. Add a piece of lemon peel.

For a Dry Manhattan, prepare same as Manhattan Cocktail, leaving out syrup.

MANHATTAN COCKTAIL—EXTRA DRY

Bitters   Whiskey
French vermouth   Lemon peel

Mix same as Manhattan Cocktail. Leave out syrup, and use French vermouth in place of Italian.

MARGUERITE COCKTAIL

Bitters   Plymouth gin   French vermouth

Take a half of mixing-glass full of fine ice, three dashes of orange bitters, one-half jigger of Plymouth gin, one-half jigger of French vermouth. Mix, strain into cocktail-glass. Place an olive in the bottom of glass and serve.

MARTINI COCKTAIL—No. 1

Bitters   Italian vermouth
Gin   Lemon peel

Fill a mixing-glass half-full of fine ice, three dashes orange bitters, one-half jigger Tom gin, one-half Italian vermouth, a piece lemon peel. Mix, strain into cocktail-glass.

MARTINI COCKTAIL—No. 2

Bitters   Sherry
Tom gin   Lemon peel
Italian vermouth

Fill mixing-glass half-full of fine ice. Add two dashes Boker's bitters, one-half jigger Tom gin, one-half Italian vermouth, half a teaspoonful sherry, piece of lemon peel. Mix and strain into cocktail-glass.

METROPOLE COCKTAIL

Syrup   French vermouth
Bitters   Lemon peel
Brandy

Half a mixing-glass half-full of fine ice, add two dashes gum-syrup, two dashes Peyschaud bitters, one dash orange bitters, half a jigger brandy, half a jigger French vermouth. Mix, strain into cocktail-glass, add small piece twisted lemon peel.

PRINCETON COCKTAIL

Bitters   Tom gin   Port wine

A mixing-glass half-full of fine ice, three dashes orange bitters, one and a half pony Tom gin. Mix, strain into cocktail-glass; add half a pony port wine carefully, and let it settle in bottom of cocktail before serving.

RIDING CLUB COCKTAIL

Bitters   Acid phosphate   Calisaya

Mixing-glass half-full of fine ice, one dash Angostura Bitters, a small bar-spoonful Horsford's acid phosphate, one jigger calisaya. Mix, and strain into cocktail-glass.

ROB ROY COCKTAIL

Bitters   Scotch whiskey
Lemon peel   Italian vermouth

Fill a mixing-glass half-full of fine ice. Add two dashes Boker's bitters, one-half jigger Scotch whiskey, one-half jigger Italian vermouth. Mix, and strain into cocktail-glass. Place a small piece lemon peel on top.

SODA COCKTAIL

Syrup   Italian vermouth
Bitters   Lemon peel
Brandy

Fill a mixing-glass half-full of fine ice, add two dashes gum-syrup, three dashes Peyschaud or Boker's bitters, one-half jigger apple brandy, one-half jigger Italian vermouth. Mix, strain into cocktail glass, twist small piece lemon peel on top.

TURF COCKTAIL

Bitters   Tom gin   Lemon peel

One dash Angostura Bitters, three dashes orange bitters, one jigger Tom gin in a mixing-glass half-full of fine ice. Mix, strain into cocktail-glass; add a piece twisted lemon peel.

VERMOUTH COCKTAIL

Bitters   Italian vermouth   Lemon peel

Mixing-glass half-full of fine ice, two dashes Boker's or Peyschaud bitters, one jigger Italian vermouth. Mix well, strain into cocktail-glass; add a piece lemon peel.

VERMOUTH COCKTAIL—DRY

Bitters   French vermouth   Lemon peel

Prepare same as Vermouth Cocktail, using French vermouth in place of Italian; twist a piece of lemon peel over top.

VERMOUTH COCKTAIL—FANCY

Maraschino   Italian vermouth
Bitters   Lemon peel

Have mixing-glass half-full of fine ice. Add three dashes maraschino, two dashes Boker's bitters, one jigger Italian vermouth and one dash orange bitters. Mix and strain into cocktail-glass, the rim of which has been moistened with a piece of lemon peel dipped in powdered sugar.

VERMOUTH COCKTAIL—FRENCH

Bitters   French vermouth   Lemon peel

Mixing-glass half-full of fine ice, two dashes gum-syrup, two dashes Peyschaud bitters, one jigger whiskey. Mix, strain into cocktail-glass; add a small piece of twisted lemon peel.

WHISKEY COCKTAIL—FANCY

Maraschino   Whiskey
Bitters   Lemon peel

Half a mixing-glass half-full of fine ice. Add two dashes maraschino, two dashes Boker's bitters, one jigger whiskey, one dash orange bitters. Mix until very cold. Strain into cocktail-glass, the rim of which has been moistened with a piece of lemon peel dipped in powdered sugar.

WHISKEY COCKTAIL—OLD-FASHIONED

Sugar   Lemon peel
Bitters   Whiskey

Put a lump of sugar in a whiskey-glass; add enough hot water to cover the sugar. Crush the sugar; add a lump of ice, two dashes Boker's bitters, small piece of lemon peel, one jigger whiskey. Mix with small bar-spoon and serve with spoon in glass.

WHISKEY COCKTAIL—NEW YORK

Bitters   Sherry
Whiskey   Lemon peel
Italian vermouth

Fill mixing-glass half-full of fine ice. Add two dashes Boker's bitters, one-half jigger whiskey, one-half jigger Italian vermouth, half a teaspoonful sherry, piece of lemon peel. Mix, strain into cocktail-glass.

YALE COCKTAIL

Bitters   Tom gin
Lemon peel   Seltzer

Fill a mixing-glass half-full of fine ice, three dashes orange bitters, one dash Peyschaud bitters, a piece lemon peel, one jigger Tom gin. Mix, strain into cocktail-glass; add a squirt from the siphon.

DRINKS

"Do as adversaries do in law, strive mightily, but eat and drink as friends."—Taming of the Shrew.

CHOCOLATE is an appropriate luncheon beverage as are malt liquors. Luncheon wines are sherry, sauterne and champagne. Claret cup may be used, or wine may be omitted altogether. Lemonades, punches and fruit drinks are used for afternoon affairs. For a supper party serve a cocktail and perhaps "cups"—claret, sherry or fruit cup. At Christmas serve eggnog, mulled wine or punch.

At dinner when wine is served it is poured from the right hand of the guest, in the intervals of the different courses. Serve sherry and Madeira with the first course at dinner, Chateau Yquem or other white wine with the fish; claret with the entree; champagne ice or champagne or Madeira with the dessert. There is no arbitrary rule for dinner wines, the custom differs in different countries.

White wines should be served cool but not iced; sherry should be the temperature of the room. Claret is served without cooling; champagne should be chilled in ice and salt for an hour before serving.

Wines are named but their use is a matter of choice. After black coffee is served in the drawing-room pass liqueurs; brandy, benedictine, chartreuse, creme de menthe, or curaçao. Later on pass Apollinaris or other charged water.

AFTERNOON PUNCH

Juice of 11 lemons	1½ cup sugar
Juice of 1 orange	1 cup boiling water
1 bunch of mint	6 pint bottles ginger ale

Stand all ingredients on ice three or four hours except ginger ale which is added with ice when served. For 16 to 18 people.

CHAMPAGNE PUNCH

1 cup water	2 tablespoons old rum
2 cups sugar	2 tablespoons Curaçao
1 quart champagne	Juice 2 lemons
4 tablespoons brandy	2 cups tea

Pour these over crushed ice. One quart soda water may be added.

CHRISTMAS TEMPERANCE PUNCH

2 baked apples	1 pint grape juice
4 lemons	1 pint ginger ale
6 oranges	1 pint soda water
4 pounds sugar	

Grate the yellow rind of the lemons and oranges and add sugar and two quarts of water. Stir until sugar is dissolved and boil ten minutes. Strain and cool, add juice of lemon and oranges and baked apples pressed through a sieve. When wanted for use put a small block of ice in the punch bowl, pour over the syrup, add grape juice, ginger ale and enough effervescent water to make it palatable.

"COCO DE AGUA" HIGHBALL

8 lumps sugar   Coco de agua   1 jigger rum

Put the lumps of sugar in a glass, dissolve with a little water; add a jigger of best rum and put in some cracked ice. Fill the glass with "coco de agua" (the water from the green cocoanut).

"COCOAGE", FROM MARTINIQUE

1 egg	Coco de agua
1 jigger rum	Sugar

To a freshly beaten egg add a jigger of best rum and sugar to taste. Put in a glass and fill it up with "coco de agua". Muddle well with a swizzlestick.

TO MAKE CORDIAL AND WINE FROM ORANGE JUICE

A sweet, pleasant cordial may be made from the juice of the sour orange. The usual formula is to add three gallons of water to one of juice of sour oranges, and then three pounds of white sugar to each gallon. After fermentation, bottle. Let stand a few months.

A formula for converting the juice of the sweet orange into wine, which is said to be worthy of the name, is as follows: Take of sweet orange juice and water equal parts, and add three pounds of pure sugar to each gallon, in a tight, full barrel, with a bent tube from a bunghole to a vessel of water. When the gas-bubbles cease to show in the water, the barrel must be closed and put away for several months, when the liquor can be drawn off, bottled and corked tightly. The bottles must be kept in a cool place till wanted for use.

CREAM OF ALMONDS
"HORCHATA DE ALMENDRAS"

Pound blanched almonds in a mortar until so finely ground they can be strained through a fine sieve by the addition of a little water. It should be of the consistency of a creamy emulsion. Add sugar to taste.

CREAM OF SESAME
"HORCHATA DE AJONJOLI"

Take sesame seeds and proceed the same as for "Horchata de Almendras".

CLARET CUP—No. 1

1 quart claret wine	1 quart apollinaris
½ cup Curaçao	Sugar
2 tablespoons brandy	Mint leaves
½ cup orange juice	

Mix with cracked ice, putting in apollinaris just before serving.

CLARET CUP—No. 2

1 bottle claret	3 slices cucumber
1 bottle any other wine	Sugar
1 wine-glass brandy	Soda
1 lemon rind cut very thin	Sprig of mint

Mix ingredients in a claret cup with sugar enough to make the cup palatable, plenty of fine ice, and, last of all, two bottles seltzer water or plain soda. Serve the claret cup as soon as it is made.

EGG LEMONADE

1 tablespoon of fine sugar	1 egg
5 dashes lemon juice	

In a large bar-glass put three-fourths glass shaved ice and the above ingredients; fill with water, stir well, strain.

EGGNOG

1 egg
1 cup evaporated milk diluted with ½ cup water

1 tablespoon sugar	Grating of nutmeg
Few grains salt	1 teaspoon strawberry jam

Beat egg and add sugar, nutmeg and salt. Add milk and stir well. Add jam and serve.

EGGNOG, IMPERIAL

1 tablespoonful sugar	1 wine-glassful brandy
1 fresh egg	½ wine-glassful Jamaica rum
⅓ glass fine ice	

Shake thoroughly in an egg-nog shaker and strain. Grate nutmeg on top. For hot egg-nog, omit ice and add hot milk to taste.

SNOWBALL

1 egg	1 pint bottle ginger ale
2 teaspoons powdered sugar	

Beat egg, stir in other ingredients. Serve in Collins' glass.

SHERRIED FRUIT DRINK

½ cup orange juice	½ cup pineapple juice
1 cup grapefruit juice	½ cup sherry

Combine chilled fruit juices with the sherry and serve.

GINGER DRINK

A Healthy Summer Drink to Satisfy Thirst.

½ cup vinegar	6 teaspoonfuls sugar
2 teaspoonfuls ginger	

To each pint of cold water mix one-half cup of good vinegar; two teaspoonfuls of ginger, and six teaspoonfuls of granulated sugar and keep covered in a cool place.

LEMON BRANDY

Have a bottle three quarters full of brandy; when you use lemons for other purposes, pare off the yellow skin very thin, cut it small and drop it in the bottle till you get it full. Be careful not to put in any of the tough white part, as that will give it a bitter taste; cork the bottle and keep it to season cakes and puddings.

MABI or MAVI *(Colubrina Reclinata)*

Mabi bark	Ginger root
1 orange peel	¾ pound sugar
Anise seeds	

The *palo mabi* is a shrub or low tree found in the mountains in all the Antilles. The wood is strong and used for building. The bark is used to make the drink called "mabi" which is cooling, appetizing and its bitter qualities make it a remedy for indigestion. The bark can be bought in market or in the "apothecary hall" as drug stores are called in some of the islands.

Take a small handful of mabi bark, the peel of one sweet orange, a pinch of anise seeds and a small "hand" of ginger root, ¾ pound of sugar and put on to boil with enough water to cover. Cook about twenty minutes and then add three quarts of water, set aside until the next day, when it will begin to "work". If you have a little left from a previous making, put it in and it will hasten the leaven. Do not cork the bottles but let the foam form on top. Put in the ice-box; an unequalled drink for warm weather and a fine stomach tonic.

MINT JULEP

Fresh mint   Brandy
Sugar   Berries

Use for an ordinary tumbler half a dozen sprigs of fresh mint; bruise the tops a little in the glass with one tablespoonful of sugar and two of water, using a teaspoon; then pour in a wine-glass and a half of brandy; take out the mint, fill the glass with shaved ice, and put the mint in again with the stems down. On the top of the julep arrange fresh berries or fruits and serve.

MISS BLYDEN

1 tablespoon sugar   Prickly pear juice
1 jigger rum

When George Washington visited the Barbadoes he partook of "Miss Blyden" and liked it so much he wrote home about it.

Dissolve sugar in a glass, add a jigger of best old rum, fill the glass with juice or prickly pear suitably iced. Prickly pear is the fruit of a cactus, *opuntia ficus indica,* sometimes called "tuna". It is filled with a juice very cooling and "saludable".

MULLED WINE

1 pint wine   Nutmeg
3 eggs   Allspice
3 tablespoons sugar

Put a pint of wine over the fire to heat with a pint of water; meantime, beat three eggs with three tablespoonfuls of sugar; when the wine is hot, but not boiling, pour it on the eggs, beating the mixture constantly; if the wine is too hot, it will curdle or cook the eggs; sweeten the mulled wine to taste, grate a little nutmeg on it, add a little allspice, and serve it hot.

MURTABERRY CORDIAL

4 quarts murtaberries   Brandy
5 pounds sugar

To four quarts of murtas put five pounds of sugar and half a gallon of water; stir this well and set away in a stone jar. Remove any scum that may have formed and add to every gallon a pint of brandy; put it in a demijohn, stopper it tightly.

ORANGE SYRUP—No. 1

Select juicy oranges in prime condition, and dissolve to each quart of juice two pounds of sugar and the juice of two good sized lemons; allow this to boil for twelve or fifteen minutes; skim clean, filter through filtering paper in funnel placed in your bottles or fruit jars, and seal air-tight.

ORANGE SYRUP—No. 2

Squeeze juice of ripe oranges through a sieve; add a pound of sugar to every pint of juice; boil slowly for ten minutes; skim carefully, bottle when cold. Two or three sponfuls of this in a glass of ice water is refreshing; it may also be used with melted butter for pudding sauce.

PINEAPPLE BRANDY

Brandy   1 ripe pineapple
Sugar

Pare a large, ripe pineapple, saving the rind to make pineapple cider, and slice it about a quarter of an inch thick; then weigh it, and use an equal weight of powdered sugar. Put the fruit and sugar in layers in a large glass jar, with sugar at the bottom and top; pour into the jar enough of the best brandy to stand an inch above the pineapple; then close the jar air-tight, and keep it in a cool, dry, dark closet for a month or longer. Use the fruit for the table; and the brandy, mixed with soda water or seltzer, for a drink in hot weather.

PINEAPPLE CIDER

Pineapple rinds   Sugar

To each pineapple rind, chopped in small pieces, add two quarts of cold water and allow to stand until it ferments, which will take about three days in warm weather; strain off the water, add about one-third pound sugar to each quart of liquid, then bottle, fasten the corks down with wire or string, allow bottles to remain lying on their sides for three days, and then it will be ready to serve.

PINEAPPLE LEMONADE

2 pounds sugar   2 pineapples
6 lemons

Boil slowly two pounds of sugar to one quart of cold water until it forms a thin syrup; skim clean. Add the juice of six large lemons, no seeds. Peel and grate pineapples into a bowl; add syrup; allow to stand for three hours, then add two quarts of ice water, mix well, strain it through cheese cloth, and it is ready to serve.

PINEAPPLE RUM

1 pineapple   Rum   1¼ pounds sugar

Select a ripe pineapple, slice it, put in a glass jar and pour over the best rum so it will be completely covered, seal jar and allow it to remain three days. Have a syrup in readiness made from one and one-quarter pounds of sugar to one pint of water. Boil syrup until it is clear, strain it through cheese cloth, and allow it to cool. Strain the liquor from the pineapple, pressing the fruit so as to extract all the juice, then mix the juice, liquor and syrup together, adding a half pint of lemon juice to same, and also about one quart more rum, and bottle for use. Use one-third of this concoction to one-third iced water for a summer drink.

PINEAPPLE SYRUP

Pineapple   Sugar

Cut the pineapple in small pieces and to each three pounds add one quart of water, boil until very soft. Mash and filter in another vessel and to each pint of syrup add from three-quarters to one pound of granulated sugar. Boil to a rich syrup, bottle and seal air-tight.

PUNCH A LA ROMAINE

2 pounds powdered sugar   12 egg whites
1 dozen lemons   1 quart champagne
2 oranges   1 quart Jamaica rum

This beverage requires to be partly frozen in an ice pail or an ice cream freezer. Mix powdered sugar in the juice of the lemons; add the thin yellow rind and the juice of two oranges and stir until the sugar is dissolved; strain the syrup and mix with it the whites of a dozen eggs beaten to a stiff froth. Freeze this mixture nearly solid; then quickly stir into it one bottle each of champagne and Jamaica rum, and serve the punch at once in small goblets or champagne glasses. The freezing mixture is composed of equal parts of salt and pounded ice packed around the vessel containing the Roman punch.

PUNCH FOR A PARTY (H. W. D.)

1 cup strong tea   ½ cup lime juice
1 cup sugar   1 cup murtaberry juice
1 bottle claret   ½ wineglass brandy
1 bottle water   ½ wineglass apricot licquer
Juice of 1 orange   ½ wineglass curaçao
½ wineglass blackberry juice

Pour over a punch bowl quite full of fine ice. The melting ice will liquify the punch sufficiently.

"REFRESCO DE PEPINO"

This is made from the large red "pepino" one sees hanging in the markets or in the vender's carts. It is a cucurbit, related to the cucumber and the melon, with a fragrance not unlike a melon. Cut the fruit into slices, press out the juice and strain it clear from the seeds. Fill a glass with chopped ice and pour the juice over it. It is refreshing and a tonic to the stomach.

ROMAN PUNCH

1 tablespoon sugar
1 tablespoon syrup
½ lemon
Berries

1 teaspoon port
1 teaspoon curaçao
1 wineglass Jamaica rum
½ wineglass brandy.

Mix above ingredients in a large tumbler. Fill the glass with shaved ice; put a teaspoonful of port wine on top, and whatever berries or fruit are in season. Drink the punch through a straw.

SAUTERNE CUP

½ orange
½ lemon
2 tablespoons curaçao
½ cup sugar

2 cups sauterne
Mint leaves
1 quart soda water.

Chip the half rinds of orange and lemon, cover with Curaçao and let stand two hours. Add sugar, sauterne, and chill. Just before serving add soda-water and garnish with mint leaves and sliced oranges.

SHERRY FLIP

½ glass fine ice
1 egg

½ teaspoon sugar
1½ wineglassfuls sherry

Shake well. Strain into a fancy glass with nutmeg on top.

SHERRY COBBLER FROZEN

1 quart sherry wine
1 quart water

Juice of six large lemons
Sugar

Sweeten very richly to the taste, add thinly cut lemon peel and freeze. It freezes very easily.

SUGAR-CANE FIELDS

From "Seven Sonnets on Puerto Rico"
GRACE SPENCER PHILLIPS

Dark, lush and fertile lies each broad plowed field
In rich, wide valley or on coastal plain.
The land waits for the tender shoots to yield
Their honeyed crop of growing sugar-cane,
Within those graceful stalks there lies concealed
A world of sweetness. Fed by gentle rain
The plants grow tall and stately, and close-sealed,
The glazéd wall the nectar does retain.

Wide flung, a sea of waving, flowing green,
That pulses as the billows at their play,
While over all the arrow bloom is seen.
Silver and lavender, it mounts like spray
To waft the golden sheen of sun-lit glow
Above the fields, as light as thistle-blow.

RUM

"There's naught, no doubt, so much the spirit calms as rum and true religion."—BYRON, *Don Juan.*

RUM is made in countries where sugar-cane grows, for it is one of the by-products of sugar. The finest rum today comes from the West Indies. Each island's product differs somewhat due to different climates and methods used in distilling and ageing. Some of the best rums are made by secret processes. The relation of the congenerics, the proportionate relation of solids or liquid essences determine both the body and quality and aroma of rum. Each manufacturer has his traditions and methods, often handed down in a family for generations.

Rum was a very common drink in the early days of colonial commerce, a part of military rations, and was provided for seamen on vessels.

Among some old letters of my grandmother's written more than a hundred years ago was one from an aunt of hers in which she said, "Uncle David is going away to the West Indies, in one of his ships, taking down potatoes and codfish, and bringing home mahogany and *rum.* We have all packed up our chintz dresses to send by him for they do such beautiful laundry work in those islands." Uncle David was a ship owner in Lynn, Massachusetts, but it was Uncle David's last trip for he died in St. Kitts and lies under a marker in the little old Anglican church there. I have always wondered if the chintz dresses got back safely.

DAIQUIRI

Juice ½ lime   1 jigger white rum   ½ teaspoon sugar
Mix and shake with shaved ice.

CUBA LIBRE

Juice ½ lime   Coca-Cola   Jigger Gold Label P.R. rum
Serve in tall glass with ice, filling glass with Coca-Cola.

JAMAICA HOT RUM

3 parts rum   6 parts hot water
1 part lime juice   Syrup to taste
3 parts brandy

Serve in china mugs.

NEW ENGLAND HOT BUTTERED RUM

Into a large pitcher put a stick of cinnamon, three ounces rum, one teaspoon
of butter. Add hot water and steep for a few minutes.

PLANTERS PUNCH

"One of sour" (lime juice)   "Three of strong" (rum)
"Two of sweet" (sugar)   "Four of weak" (water and ice)
                Dash of angostura
Shake well in tall glass with ice.

HAITIAN FLIP

1 egg   1 teaspoon sugar   1 jigger of rum
Shake with ice, sprinkle with nutmeg.

BARBADOES SWIZZLE

4 teaspoons sugar   Sprig fresh mint
Juice 6 limes   1 pint rum

Mix in tall pitcher with eight cubes of ice. Stir well and serve.

JAMAICA RUM COCKTAIL

Syrup   Jamaica rum
Bitters   Lemon peel

Mixing-glass half-full of fine ice, two dashes gum-syrup, two dashes orange
bitters, two dashes Boker's bitters, one jigger Jamaica rum. Mix and strain
into cocktail-glass. Add a small piece twisted lemon peel.

MEDFORD RUM COCKTAIL

Syrup   Medford rum
Bitters   Lemon peel

Have a mixing-glass half-full of fine ice. Add a dash of gum-syrup, two dashes Boker's bitters, one jigger Medford rum. Mix and strain into a glass. Add a piece of twisted lemon peel.

SWIZZLES are mixed drinks typical of the West Indies. They are usually compounded with rum as the principal ingredient, although gin or brandy or bitters are also used. But the virtue of the drink lies in its being mixed with a swizzle-stick which not only beats the drink to a froth, but imparts its own flavor to the drink. The stick is from a plant, the main stem of which at the root separates into roots which spread like the spokes of a wheel. The stick is cut so that the main stem is about ten or twelve inches long, the spokes about an inch. Held upright in a glass the stem is rapidly rotated between one's two palms. The Spaniards used a similar stick, on the same principle, to mull chocolate into creamy consistency, although this stick is larger. These chocolate sticks were formerly to be found in the shops. Some were elaborately carved, a real ornament to the kitchen and fun to use. Many families cherish their antique chocolate "mills" as a prized possession handed down from a remote grandmother or great-grandmother.

CACAO OR CHOCOLATE

"Youth and age their cocoa cherish,
Sent by God mankind to nourish."—Anon.

THE cacao tree is a wild plant of the western hemisphere and like tobacco was not known to Europe until after the discovery of America. The Spaniards found it in use in Mexico by the Aztecs. Bags of cacao containing a certain number of beans were used in exchange in place of currency. The cacao was introduced into Spain and from there to other parts of Europe. The *Public Advertiser* of London in 1657 had an announcement that "In Bishopgate St. at a Frenchman's house is an excellent West Indian drink called chocolate, to be sold, where you may have it ready at any time, and also unmade at reasonable rates." Chocolate soon became a very fashionable drink.

The plant has rather thin leaves, and the pods are borne on the trunk of the tree or on the branches. The similarity of names of cocoa and cacao has led to some confusion; cocoa butter is the product of the cacao and should not be confused with coconut oil which comes from the coconut. Unfortunately *coconut* is sometimes spelled *cocoanut* which is confusing. The terms of cocoa and chocolate leads one to think they are separate entities while as a matter of fact cocoa is the ground cacao bean after the fat has been removed from the bean. Bitter chocolate is the firm mass obtained by grinding the bean without removing any of the fat.

In tea and coffee we drink the infusion of the leaves or seed while in cocoa the whole is taken in a state of suspension. As a beverage it has a similar action to tea and coffee.

COCOA

Take 1½ teaspoons cocoa, 2 teaspoons sugar, a little salt, mix with enough cold water to blend. Add to ½ cup evaporated milk and ½ cup water in double boiler. Cook three minutes, beat and serve.

COCOA SHELLS

Put a teacupful of shells to a quart of boiling water. Soak overnight and boil well. Scald a pint of milk and add.

CHOCOLATE No. 1

Scald 3 cups milk; melt 1½ squares of unsweetened chocolate in a saucepan placed over a teakettle; add 4 level tablespoonfuls sugar, a few grains of salt, and gradually 1½ cups boiling water. Stir until smooth. Boil one minute. Then add to the scalded milk and beat with the egg beater 2 minutes. Serve in chocolate cups with or without whipped cream.

CHOCOLATE No. 2

(ST. THOMAS)

Allow a square of sweet chocolate to a cupful of milk. Scrape and mix the chocolate to a fine paste with a little water. Then put it to boil with the milk and let it boil up three times. It should be muddled all the time, with a muddling stick.

BRANDY COCOA

Make cocoa by using 1½ teaspoons of cocoa, 1½ teaspoons sugar, 3 table-spoons boiling water and ⅔ cupful scalded milk. Just at serving add a scant tablespoonful of brandy.

COFFEE

"After the coffee things ain't so bad."—That Inside Song.

COFFEE was apparently first used in Aden as a beverage. The Arabs called coffee "kawa" and knew its beneficial action; they also utilized the leaves and shells of the berries. It was introduced into Europe, appearing in Venice in 1615, and its popularity rapidly spread throughout the continent. Until 1690 the world's supply came from Arabia and Abyssinia. It is said that coffee was first brought to Puerto Rico late in the 17th century. With its drooping branches laden with delicate white blossoms and shiny green leaves, the coffee is one of the most lovely of agricultural plants. Later when the blossoms fall and bright red "cherries" take their place, it is equally beautiful. In Puerto Rico the processes are carried on by hand. The women and children go down into the *fincas* (plantations) with their baskets and pick the red berries. They are run through a machine that takes off the outer skin. Every berry has two halves held together by pulp, excepting the pea berry or *caracolillo* which is greatly prized here. The enclosing pulp is sweet and has to be soaked off. Then the coffee is spread on great wooden trays or on cement "glacis" or pavement to dry in the sun and raked for days with flat wooden rakes. In order to remove the parchment from the beans, after being hulled it is winnowed. In small farms these processes are quite primitive. The coffee is roasted over an open fire and used freshly ground. It is believed in the mountains of Puerto Rico that coffee powdered with a pestle and mortar of *guayacan* (lignum vitæ) is far superior to that ground in an ordinary wooden mill.

TO ROAST COFFEE

Dry the coffee in the oven an hour or two before roasting. When ready to roast, put it in a round-bottomed kettle (iron) and stir it constantly until browned. Add a small piece of butter just before taking it up. Put it while steaming hot into a box with a tight cover. Grind as wanted.

CAFE NOIR

Nothing more delectable in the way of coffee can be imagined than the native coffee, properly made; it should be freshly roasted and pulverized and made by pouring boiling water over a bag containing the coffee in the proportion of a tablespoon of the pulverized coffee to a ½ cup of boiling water.

ICED COFFEE

Twelve ounces of sugar, 1 pint of water, 1 pint of black coffee, 1 quart of cream. Boil the sugar and water together for five minutes, then add the coffee, then the cream, and when cold freeze. Serve in tall glasses.

COFFEE EXTRACT

Use 2 tablespoons of powdered coffee to ½ cup boiling water. Pour through a coffee bag and let drip three times. This is convenient to carry traveling when hot milk may be ordered and the extract added to it.

BREAKFAST COFFEE

Take 1 tablespoon powdered coffee to 1 cup of boiling water. Pour through a coffee bag and let drip. Heat same quantity milk and pour the coffee and milk simultaneously into a warm cup. This is called *café con leche* (coffee with milk).

A coffee bag may be made by taking a triangle of cotton flannel, joining the seams so it forms a cornucopia and at the top put a narrow hem to put a wire through. Bend it into a circle twisting the ends of the wire into a handle. Scald it to take away any taste of the cloth before using. This bag holds the powdered coffee, and boiling water is slowly poured through. After using wash the bag in fresh water, (no soap) and hang in the sun to air.

Coffee made in this way is delicious.

TEA

Tea is extensively used as a beverage by continentals and Europeans in the island. The native-born use it to break up colds. Years ago it could only be bought in the drug stores. No recipes are given for they can be found in any cookbook.

SOUPS

"Now good digestion, wait on appetite, and health on both."
                                                    —Macbeth.

THERE is magic in the soup-pot. Nothing is so satisfying and nourishing as a good plate of soup, nothing is easier to make than good soup, once one learns to make it. It adds something of value to every meal used. A spoonful of peas, a bit of left over potatoes, a tomato, a stalk of celery, a spoonful of gravy, all can be worked up into a delicious soup when creamed or added to stock, which may be prepared in quantity, kept in the ice-box and used as required. A dozen raisins or a few good prunes added to soup a half hour before it is done, makes it delicious. Use seasoning sparingly in stock that is strongly flavored, and in any soup do not combine too many vegetables as the flavor will be impaired, but in the more tasteless soups add celery, salt, onion juice, Worcestershire sauce or catsup. For utensils in soup making one needs only a covered kettle, bowls to keep stock in, a wooden spoon, a ladle, and a coarse strainer of wire. In making soups with milk cook the ingredients with a little water and add heated milk afterwards.

RED BEAN SOUP

½ lb. red kidney beans	Garlic
1 onion	1 cup evaporated milk
Pork or bacon	1 tablespoon butter
1 cup tomatoes	1 tablespoon flour

Soak red kidney beans overnight in water to cover. Put on to simmer or cook in fireless cooker. Pass through puree strainer. Fry an onion with small pieces of pork or bacon, adding a cup of tomatoes, tiny pieces of garlic, salt and pepper. Add to puree with one cup evaporated milk thickened with one tablespoon butter, and one tablespoon flour. Serve piping hot with croutons.

JELLIED BOUILLON

1 pound veal	2 ounces barley
1 pound beef	

Put veal, beef and pearl barley into a quart of cold water and let them boil down to a pint. Rub all through a sieve. Melt a spoonful of this strengthening jelly when required. It will keep indefinitely in an ice-box and is especially good for convalescents.

OLD ISABEL'S BOUILLON

3 pounds beef	1 can tomatoes
Ham and veal bones	2 heads celery
3 onions	Parsley
2 eggs	Cloves
3 carrots	

Cut lean beef into pieces the size of dice; add two gallons of water, a ham bone and some veal bones. Simmer for three hours. Remove any scum or grease, add onions, carrots, tomatoes, celery, two pepper pods, two cloves, a sprig of parsley. Return to the fire and cook until vegetables are tender. Strain into a large bowl and let cool. When ready to serve place in a saucepan with two well-beaten eggs, stir until it boils; then strain again and serve.

TO BROWN SUGAR FOR A SOUP

Take two large spoonfuls of brown sugar; put it in a pan over the fire. Let it melt and add half a pint of water; let it boil. One large spoonful will brown a soup. This is also the mode of preparing the browning of caramel ice cream.

CHICKEN BROTH

Chicken	2 tablespoons rice
Small onion	

Cut a chicken up fine, break the bones. Put in a saucepan with two quarts of water, a small onion, salt and two tablespoonfuls of rice. When it boils skim carefully, cover and let cook a long time.

CHICKEN SOUP

1 hen	Small bunch parsley
2 onions	Bacon
1 carrot	1 cup milk

One large old chicken cut into pieces, put on in a quart of water. Throw in onions, parsley, carrot, and a small piece of lean bacon. Let them boil half an hour, then reduce the heat and let simmer a long time. Take off the soup, stir it and if there is much grease, skim it. Chop a cupful of the white meat very fine, put it in a tureen with minced parsley and pour the soup over this, adding a cup of milk.

CONSOMMÉ

4 pounds beef	1 stalk celery
1 ounce suet	1 egg-white
1 small carrot	1 onion

Cut into dice, lean beef from the round; put about one ounce of suet and one small sliced onion into soup kettle and cook until brown; then add the meat, cooking without covering thirty minutes; cover with cold water; cover the kettle and simmer gently for about three hours. Add the cloves, carrot, a piece of celery and simmer one hour longer. Strain and stand away to cool. When cold remove all grease from the surface, turn the consommé into a kettle, beat the white of an egg with a half cupful of cold water, add it to the boiling consommé Boil one minute and strain through cheesecloth. Season to taste. If not dark, add a teaspoonful of caramel.

CREOLE SOUP

6 turnips	1 tablespoon butter
1 can tomatoes	1 sliced onion
2 tablespoons sweet red peppers	1 clove garlic
½ teaspoon allspice	Baking soda
1 teaspoon salt	Cream sauce

Wash and slice turnips; add tomatoes, minced sweet red peppers, allspice, one teaspoon of salt, onion, garlic and butter. Cook until the vegetables are tender, then press them through a colander. Make a cream sauce in a double-boiler (baño Maria) by stirring a tablespoon flour moistened with cream, into a pint of milk. When it boils and thickens add the vegetable puree, stirring in a pinch of soda to prevent curdling. Serve immediately, hot.

"FRIJOLE" SOUP
(DRIED BLACK-EYED BEAN SOUP)

Pick and soak overnight a pound of frijoles; strain, measure, add four times as much cold water. To each quart of water add half onion. Simmer slowly until soft. Rub through sieve. Return to fire, season with salt and pepper. Thicken each quart with one teaspoon each of butter and flour. Boil up again for a few minutes. Black-eyed bean soup should also have a pinch of mustard and a little lemon juice added, and slices of hard-boiled eggs.

"GANDULE" SOUP
(PIGEON PEA SOUP)

1 cup gandules	Bacon
1 tomato	Butter
1 onion	1 cupful squash
1 green pepper	

Stew "gandules" with a tomato. Fry an onion and a pepper with a piece of bacon and add to the "gandules"; strain through a colander; add a piece of butter, pepper and salt to taste, and mash into it a cupful of cooked squash.

SOUP FROM MAYAGUEZ

1 pint okra	2 tablespoons cassava or rice flour
1 cup carrots	Tobasco sauce
½ cup green peas	Leeks or onions
1 can tomatoes	Mace

Make a stock by boiling a pint of chopped okra in two quarts of water. Strain, add chopped carrots, chopped leeks or young onions, half green peas, salt and pepper to taste. Let this stand overnight, then add tomatoes, a blade of mace, cassava flour or rice flour, a drop of Tobasco sauce.

OKRA GUMBO

1 fat chicken	2 pods red pepper
1 tablespoon flour	½ can tomatoes
1 tablespoon lard	1 pound okra
1 slice ham	Rice
1 onion	

Stir together in a saucepan a tablespoonful of flour and one of pure lard. Chop an onion, and cut up a fat chicken into small pieces and put them in. Stir until the chicken is nearly done. When well browned, add ham cut up small; red pepper, and salt to taste. Add a quart of boiling water and leave to simmer on the stove for two hours. Slice the okra, put in a pan with a little water and simmer fifteen minutes, stirring all the time. Then add tomatoes and cook uncovered for about an hour, then cover. When the gumbo has cooked two hours let it cool and skim. Put it back on the fire, add okra and let it cook again until the okra is thoroughly done. Serve hot with dry boiled rice.

ONION SOUP
(SRA. LEDESMA)

1 cup shelled almonds	1 cup grated cheese
1 quart stock	Toast
1 cupful onions	

Pound a cupful of shelled almonds to a paste and add to a quart of stock. Chop onions until there is a cupful; fry to a light brown; add to the stock. Cover the bottom of a tureen with thin slices of toasted bread, then a cupful grated cheese. Strain the hot soup and pour into tureen.

OX-TAIL SOUP

1 oxtail	½ cup celery and onions
1 quart stock	1 teaspoon Worcestershire sauce
½ cup carrots	1 teaspoon lemon juice
½ cup turnips	Rice

Cook ox-tail, a quart of plain stock, carrot, turnip, celery and onion, one teaspoon salt, a pepper corn. When the meat falls from the bone, remove and strain. Add the Worcestershire sauce and lemon juice last. Keep the meat for hash. Serve little moulds of hot rice with the soup, and if in season, aguacates cut in dice.

TO IMPROVE ANY SOUP

To thicken white or fish soups, pour them hot on the well-beaten yolks of two or three eggs.

PORTUGUESE SOUP

1 onion	Stale bread
1 can tomatoes	Parmesan cheese

Slice an onion and stew it. Add tomatoes and bring to a boil. Pour over stale bits of bread in a tureen in which Parmesan cheese has been grated.

"PUCHERO," OR SPANISH "POT AU FEU"

2 carrots	1 pound ham
2 onions	2 pounds soup beef
1 teaspoon thyme	½ fowl
1 stalk celery	1½ cup parboiled beans
1 bunch parsley	½ small cabbage
1 pint okra pods	1 head lettuce

Chop fine one pound of lean ham; cut into two-inch dice two pounds of soup beef; one-half a good sized fowl, or one small chicken, cut into pieces and browned in butter. Add one cup and one-half of parboiled dried beans. Put all into a soup pot; pour over them water enough to cover, and simmer for two hours. Add cabbage, lettuce, sliced carrots, sliced onions, dried thyme, celery cut into one-inch pieces, and parsley. Let simmer for an hour, then add a pint of okra pods, and cook until these are soft. If chicken, instead of fowl, is used, this should not be added until time to add the vegetables. To serve, strain off the soup into a tureen, and serve the meats and vegetables on a platter, garnished with duchesse potatoes and rings of sweet red pepper.

TRES CUARTOS DE HORA

2 pounds beef	Celery
3 carrots	Parsley
2 onions	½ can tomatoes
Cabbage	Macaroni

Cut off the fat of a round of beef very carefully, put in a saucepan and add cold water to cover well. Put the cover on half way to allow steam to evaporate, simmer and skim as scum arises. Prepare carrots, onions, a small piece of cabbage, a piece of celery, parsley and pepper pod. Put them in the broth with tomatoes and cook for two hours, skimming it carefully. It can be strained and served clear, or with rice, vermicelli or macaroni. It is also served with a poached egg added to each plate of soup, with a square of toasted bread.

TURTLE SOUP
To Dress a Turtle for Soup
(A very old recipe from Barbados)

Cut off the head and hang it with the body to bleed. When the bleeding has stopped, place the turtle on its back, and with a sharp knife separate the back from the under shell; take off the fins; break up the under shell and put it in a pan with the fins, pour boiling water over it; let it stand until it is soft enough to pull off the tough skin; put them to soak in salt and water. Clean the inwards; separate the heart, liver and light from the gall, and put them with the sweetbreads into salt and water, after having cleaned them thoroughly; clean the meat and green fat from the top shell; put them all into water and let remain overnight.

To Make the Soup

Halve a calf's head thoroughly cleaned, take out the brains and clean the head, put it in cold water to soak two hours. Wash all the turtle and put that into cold water. Put the turtle meat and the calf's head into a pot, cover with cold water and let it boil all day. Put the heart, liver and sweetbread of the turtle into a cloth and put to boil with the rest for three hours; use them to make forcemeat balls, strain the soup, set it with the meat away in a cool place till the next morning. Put into a large pot half a pound of butter and four large onions, cut fine; fry a nice brown, take off the pot, add a tablespoonful of ground clove, one of allspice, one of mace, two of nutmeg and one of pepper, two of salt, two of sweet pepper, two of summer-savory, two of chopped parsley, stir this together, then add the soup and set it on to boil. Take out all the little bones of the meat; put all into the soup, let it boil four hours. While the soup is boiling, chop up fine the liver, lights, sweetbreads and heart; add one cupful of bread-crumbs, yolks of four hard-boiled eggs, a teaspoonful of ground cloves, one of mace, one of thyme, one of summer-savory, one of sweet marjoram, one of pepper and one of salt; drop in two raw eggs and half a pound of butter. Mix it well with the hands, and make into balls the size of a pigeon's egg; roll in egg and crumbs and fry in hot fat, put on brown paper to dry and keep hot. Chop six hard-boiled eggs, cut up six or eight limes into small pieces; put a quarter of this and a quarter of the balls into each tureen; add to the soup a quart of Madeira and a quart of red wine; give it one boil; dip it into the tureen, upon the lemon, eggs, and force-meat balls and send it to the table very hot. This will make four gallons of soup.

(These directions are for a turtle weighing fifty pounds in the shell.)

KNUCKLE OF VEAL SOUP

Knuckle of veal	Parsley
2 carrots	4 cloves
3 onions	1 tablespoon brown sugar
14 allspice	½ tumbler Madeira wine

To a small knuckle of veal put carrots, onions, allspice, cloves, pepper and salt and a little chopped parsley, and two quarts water. Let it boil down well and strain. Put again on the fire and stir in two or three tablespoonfuls of browned flour, making the soup the consistency of a rich gruel. Then stir in one tablespoonful of brown sugar and a half tumbler of Madeira wine. Let it simmer for half an hour and serve.

VEGETABLE SOUP

1 soup bone	1 potato
2 tomatoes	1 onion
1 bunch okra	1 small piece cabbage
1 piece macaroni	

Cover the soup bone with two quarts of water, simmer for two hours. Add the vegetables, cook half hour. Mash the vegetables into the soup stock and strain.

FISH

"The pleasant angling is to see the fish
Cut with her golden oars the silver stream."

THE meat of fish is next in importance to that of birds and mammals. It is cheaper than other meat and very easily digested. It deserves a more important place in our diet, especially since these waters abound with fish; it is said that the waters of Tropical America are the richest field known, for more than 1,300 varieties of fish are caught on the surface. Some are sought by net or seines and others in pots. Gar, barracuda, dolphin, Spanish mackerel, salmon, bass or tarpon, mullet, bonito, fries, snapper, grouper, butterfish, porge, pargo, manchego and yellow tail are only a few of the excellent table fish.

TO SKIN, BONE AND FILLET A FISH

With a sharp knife remove fins along the back, taking off a piece of skin the entire length of back. Loosen skin from bone part of gills; when once started it can easily be drawn off. Turn the fish and skin the other side the same way. If you wish to remove bones, after skinning run the big knife close to backbone the entire length of bone, remove from one side, turn and proceed the same way on that side.

To fillet fish, skin, bone and cut into cutlets or slices. The flesh of fish should be firm, and the eyes and gills are bright in fresh fish. After dressing fish, put it in a pan covered with a cheesecloth dipped in lime or lemon juice and its odor will then not permeate the ice-box.

To fry fish, wipe dry, sprinkle with salt, dip in flour, egg and crumbs and fry in deep fat. Or dip in milk and cornmeal. Small fish are nice fried with bacon.

To bake a pompano, remove head and tail, use no water in pan; baste with butter and send to table in same dish the fish is baked in.

Sweet potatoes are especially nice with fish.

Always serve grated coconut with fish.

FISH STOCK

Save head, tail and bones of fish to make a stock, adding an onion, a carrot, a piece of celery cut up, parsley, salt and pepper, 2 cloves, ½ bay leaf, a tablespoon vinegar and water to cover. Use this bouillon instead of water for fish sauces.

FISH SOUP

1 pound fish	Toast squares
1 onion	Lime
Parsley	Hard-boiled egg
Salt and pepper	

Cut a pound of fresh fish in small pieces, add a quart of water, an onion cut up fine. When fish is well cooked, strain off the broth, reheat the broth with the addition of a tablespoon chopped parsley, salt and pepper. Cut bread into small squares, toast in the oven, put a couple of tablespoons of it in each soup plate with a thin slice of lime and grated hard-boiled egg.

BOILED FISH

Fish	Cucumbers	¼ cup butter
Onion	Parsley	½ cup flour
Carrot	Bay leaf	Evaporated milk
Lemon	Pepper corns	½ cup capers

Boil your fish, flavoring with a sliced onion, carrot and a little lemon juice. Add salt to taste. Drain well and garnish with boiled cucumbers quartered, parsley, and slices of lemon. Boil bones and head of fish with one slice onion, one slice carrot, small bay leaf, sprig of parsley, six pepper corns, half teaspoon salt, for twenty minutes. Strain. Prepare fourth cup butter creamed with half cup flour, add one cup water and evaporated milk scalded together, the fish stock and half cup capers. Serve this sauce in hot gravy dish.

FISH IN SHELLS

Fish	1 egg yolk
1 tablespoon oil	1 tablespoon butter
1 onion	1 tablespoon minced parsley
1 tablespoon flour	Cracker-crumbs

Boil a fish. In a frying pan put a tablespoonful of oil, an onion chopped fine, when brown add a tablespoonful of flour, a tablespoonful of butter, half a cup of milk and the yolk of an egg beaten. When it thickens add to it the fish in small pieces, the bones removed, and a tablespoonful of minced parsley. Grease shells or molds, put in the creamed fish; cover with rolled cracker-crumbs and brown in the oven.

DANISH FISH PUDDING

(From the Misses Quinn, St. Croix)

Fish	1 tablespoon lime juice	Hard-boiled eggs
Parsley	1 tablespoon butter	Lemon
Onion	2 tablespoons flour	Milk
Tomato	4 eggs	Capers
Pepper and salt		Paprika

Remove bones from fish, grind with parsley, onion, tomato, salt and pepper. Stir into the mixture, the lime juice, butter, flour, and four beaten eggs. Add a little milk to moisten. Mould and cook over boiling water one and a half hours.

Make a lemon sauce with capers and garnish with hard-boiled eggs sliced, paprika, slices of lemon and parsley.

FISH WITH CUCUMBER SAUCE

1 pound fish	2 cucumbers
1 tablespoon butter	Salt, pepper and vinegar

Wipe fish, cut ½ inch thick, and season with salt and pepper. Melt butter and sauté the fish, cooking it by turning frequently for 7 minutes. Grate cucumbers and drain from their liquor. Season with salt, pepper and vinegar to suit the taste.

FRESH FISH CROQUETTES

Left-over fish or 1 pound can of salmon	1 heaping tablespoon flour
Salt and cayenne pepper	½ cup cream or milk
1 teaspoon lemon juice	Yolk of egg
Scant ½ tablespoon shortening	Bread-crumbs

Take the remnants of boiled or fried fish with all skin and bone removed, or drain the oil from a pound can of salmon. Mince fine, add a half teaspoonful of salt, a dash of cayenne pepper, a teaspoonful of lemon juice. Set a scant half tablespoonful of shortening over the fire; when it begins to bubble add a heaping tablespoonful of flour and stir until the flour is cooked but not browned, then add a gill (½ cup) of cream or milk, and lastly the fish, stirring until all is smooth. If too thick add a little more milk. Make into pear shapes with a wine glass for mould, moisten with yolk of egg, roll in bread-crumbs and fry.

RICE WITH FISH

½ pound fish	Salt
Parsley	¼ cup olive oil
½ can tomato sauce	¾ cup rice
1 clove garlic, ground	Garlic
6 small onions	

Make a stock by boiling the fish in four quarts of water and straining. Add the parsley, salt, a little tomato sauce, 2 onions cut in four pieces. Cook and strain again. Take the fish off the bones, break the fish into small pieces to add to the rice afterward.

Sofrito: Cut up three or four onions very fine. Add the rest of the tomato sauce, the garlic, cook in olive oil, add to the fish broth with a bay leaf. Cook the rice in this broth, then add the pieces of fish.

COLD FISH FOR SUNDAY NIGHT

3 pounds red snapper	Parsley
2 green peppers	Thyme
2 onions	1 clove garlic
2 tomatoes	½ cup olive oil
2 stalks celery	1 tablespoon flour
1 egg-yolk	

Mince finely together green peppers, onions, tomatoes and celery. Add a bit of parsley, thyme, 1 clove garlic, salt and pepper. Cook slowly in half cup olive oil a few minutes. Slice a three-pound red snapper and lay in to cook. Pour over a little water. While it is cooking stir up the yolk of an egg, a tablespoon flour with a little water. When the fish is done remove it to a platter. Pour the egg sauce into the pot and let it cook. Strain and pour over the fish. Set it aside to cool and serve for supper with vegetable salad.

CRABS WITH RICE

In the West Indies the violet land-crab comes out of his home once a year at night and migrates to the seashore where he sheds his shell and bathes. The crabs gather together in an army and can be heard some distance as they scuttle through the bush. Then the people take torches of resinous woods to light their way and hunt the crabs. The slaughtered crabs are shelled and cooked, the favorite way is to stew them with rice. When Drake attacked the Spanish in Santo Domingo in 1597, the Englishmen lay in ambush waiting to attack. Suddenly came a rush of cavalry (as they thought) and they ran in confusion to their boats. It was in reality the army of crabs migrating, the noise in the leaves sounding like horses.

1 dozen crabs	2 carrots
1 cup rice	1 tablespoon butter
2 onions	Salt and pepper.

Clean the crabs, crush the legs and boil in salted water for an hour. Strain and skim the broth and pour it over the well washed rice. Let it stand soaking for half an hour, then cook until the rice is tender. Chop the onions and carrots, brown them in the butter, then add the crab meat. Season, add the rice and cook together ten minutes. Serve piping hot.

CRABS (LAND CRABS)

1 quart of white crab meat	2 cloves garlic
¾ cup dry sherry (Amontillado or Oloroso)	2 hard-boiled eggs
1 small cup brandy	2 teaspoons Worcestershire sauce
2 onions	Salt

Fry the onions in olive oil, add the crab meat, wine and other ingredients, leave a short time to cook gently. Last of all add the eggs cut in small pieces.

FRIED PORGIES

2 pounds porgies	¼ pound sliced bacon
Salt and pepper	Lemon slices

Clean and wash porgies, season with salt and pepper, roll them in flour and fry in bacon fat. Before frying the fish, fry sliced bacon until it is crisp and golden brown. Remove bacon and drain on brown paper until it is needed. When the fish have been browned on both sides and thoroughly done, arrange on serving platter, garnish with the crisp bacon and four slices of lemon.

CODFISH—"BACALAO"

It seems an anachronism to eat salt codfish in a country where the waters abound in fresh fish. However, in the mountainous districts it is not possible to get the fresh deep-sea fish, and codfish has been one of the cheap sustaining foods of the country since early times. We know that the early Portuguese, Spanish and English in the sixteenth century were all interested in the fisheries off the New England coast and that dried cod was a staple article of diet. The conflict between England and Spain was carried on during the reign of Queen Elizabeth, not only for the ascendency on the Spanish Main but for the northern fisheries.

Codfish is a valuable source of protein for low income groups.

The word "bacalao" is derived from the Latin word bacalum, meaning stick or stake. In both Spain and Portugal they drove the opened and flattened cod through with wooden stakes, then into the ground, so that the cod dried sail-like, in the open air. So, literally, "bacalao" or "bacalado" meant "staked."

In the small stores these dried sheets of cod spread sail-like and hung up conveniently at hand to have small quantities cut off for the purchasers, are a familiar sight in Latin countries.

SPANISH CODFISH
(From Vizcaya)

Codfish	¼ teaspoon cinnamon
1 onion	Pinch hot pepper
1 tomato	Wineglass white wine or sherry
1 teaspoon minced parsley	

Soak codfish in cold water overnight, remove bones and cut in small pieces. Put in a saucepan to stew. Add a "sofrito" prepared separately by frying an onion and a tomato chopped together, minced parsley, cinnamon, a bit of hot pepper. When cooked add to the codfish and just before serving add white wine or sherry.

SERENATA

Codfish	Yam
Sweet onions	Sweet potato
Tomatoes	Green and yellow plantain
Sweet pepper	Banana
Oil and vinegar	"Lerenes"
Salt and pepper	½ cup olive oil
Tanier	

Soak codfish overnight, then parboil, remove skin and bones. Arrange on a platter, cover with sliced sweet onions, sliced tomatoes, a small garnish of minced sweet pepper. Cover the whole with dressing made of oil, vinegar, salt and pepper. Let stand.

Boil together a piece of tanier, yam, sweet potato, green plantain, yellow plantain, banana and "lerenes." Salt well, drain off the water they were boiled in, throw over half cup of olive oil, serve hot with the codfish.

PICKLED FISH

1½ pounds fish	1½ tablespoons vinegar
2 tablespoons salt	6 tablespoons flour
1½ onions	1½ cup olive oil
4 bay leaves	4 cloves of garlic

Dress the fish using lemon juice, cover with flour and salt. Put the onion on to fry in a few tablespoons lard or substitute, adding the garlic, bay leaves and vinegar. Pour this over the fish and add a small bottle of olives and the olive oil. Cook until done. Put away in the ice-box until the next day. Serve cold.

THACKERAY'S BOUILLABAISSE

1 pound fresh fish or 1 pound canned salmon
½ cup olive oil
1 tablespoon chopped onion
2 cloves
1 peppercorn
Bay leaf
Salt

3 slices lemon
1 pint tomatoes
1 salt-spoon curry powder
½ cup white wine
Toast

The following dish was made famous by Thackeray who partook of it in Marseilles. It is popular now in Puerto Rico.

Take one-half cupful olive oil, add chopped onion, cloves, peppercorn; when this has browned add one pound of fresh fish or one can of salmon with its liquid. Add a little salt, a bay leaf, lemon, tomato, curry powder, white wine and, if needed, water to cover the fish. Simmer for twenty minutes. Line a dish with toast, remove seasoning from pan and pour the mixture over the toast.

TO FRY FRESH FISH

Fish that are to be fried should first be laid in a cloth for an hour, that the moisture may be absorbed. Scald the fish, wash and drain; cut slits on the sides of each, dredge with corn flour, season with salt and pepper, fry lightly on both sides.

TO BAKE FISH

Butter a large tin pan of sides and bottom; then put salt and pepper on the fish. Pour cream over it. Flour it well, season with salt and pepper, a few cloves and butter. Bake in hot good oven until done, then put the fish in a dish and pour the gravy over it.

Baked Fish should be accompanied by white sauce with chopped hard-boiled eggs, or drawn butter sauce.

FISH STUFFING

1 cup cracker-crumbs
¼ cup melted butter
¼ teaspoon salt

⅛ teaspoon pepper
Few drops of onion juice

1 teaspoon each of finely chopped parsley, capers and pickles.

FISH A LA PUERTO RICO
(From Margarita)

2 pounds fish
1 pound tomato
2 onions
4 cloves of garlic

2 tablespoons salt
5 tablespoons lard
1 tablespoon vinegar
1 tablespoon flour

Fry the fish in the lard, cut up the tomato and onion and fry with the garlic and vinegar, then add the fish. Prepare the flour in half cup of water and add to the mixture, put a cover on and let stew slowly.

MEAT AND FOWL

"Meat eaten without either mirth or music is ill of digestion."
—SCOTT, *The Monastery.*

SUCKLING PIG

THOROUGHLY clean the interior of a small, tender, suckling pig, reserving the liver; drain well. Season the interior with two pinches of salt, one good pinch of pepper and the third of a pinch of grated nutmeg. Chop up the liver very fine, and fry it in a saucepan with half an ounce of butter for five minutes. Stuff the pig with some forcemeat, then sew up the aperture with a kitchen needle. Have a roasting pan ready, sprinkle into it half a cupful of cold water, then lay in the pig so that it rests on its four legs, folded under. Completely cover all around with a buttered paper, then put it into a moderate oven, and let cook for two hours; baste it frequently, while cooking, with its own gravy. Remove to a hot dish, skim the fat from the gravy, and strain the lean part over the pig. Serve with hot sauce in a separate bowl.

TO ROAST A PIG (LECHON ASADO)

Month old or younger pig	Sage and sweet marjoram
2 cups bread-crumbs	1 onion
Salt and pepper	Butter
Salt pork	2 eggs
	Milk

One of the nicest forms of entertainment in an open climate is the outdoor pig roast. A charcoal pit is made, the pig impaled on a long stick which rests upon fork-shaped supports driven into the ground, so that the pig can be slowly turned over the coals and gradually roasted. It is continually basted with a sauce until thoroughly done, of a golden brown in color.

It should not be more than a month old; it is better a little less. Clean it thoroughly and sprinkle fine salt over it an hour before roasting. Take bread-crumbs, salt, pepper, sage, sweet marjoram, an onion chopped fine, butter, two eggs and a little salt pork, moistened with a little milk, stuff the pig with this and sew it up. When placed on the spit, confine the legs so as to preserve a good shape.

Rub it all over with olive oil to keep it from blistering; flour it a little at first; as soon as it begins to brown, dredge on more flour. Turn the spit every three or four minutes. If the flour falls off constantly, renew it. When it has become a dark brown color, scrape it off and set it aside. Baste the pig very often until it is done, which is when the eyes fall out. A pig weighing nine pounds requires four hours to roast. While the pig is roasting boil the feet and liver. Chop the liver, add the brains which are taken out and chopped, and the gravy thickened with the browned flour taken from the pig. A very small pig will roast in two hours and a half. Always serve fried green plantain with pig. Young goats are delicious cooked in the same manner.

AJILIMÓJILI SAUCE FOR ROAST PIG

1 tablespoon salt	½ garlic crown (that is half the cloves
1 teaspoon black pepper	from one crown of garlic)
6 peppercorns	Red hot pepper
1 cup olive oil	1 cup lemon juice

Pound together in a mortar, then add enough water to strain it all. Add olive oil and lemon juice. Use to baste the pig while roasting.

TO BAKE A HAM

Choose a nice ham, let it soak in cold water for ten hours, then wipe it dry. Cut off all poor spots and cover with a thick paste made of flour and water. Set in moderately heated oven, and bake for five hours; when done, take off the crust and peel the skin off carefully. Serve it glazed, and garnish with cut-up vegetables.

ALBONDIGAS (MEAT BALLS)

Chop ½ pound lean raw beef fine, using a meat chopper if you have one. Season to taste with salt, pepper and a few drops of onion juice. Make in small balls without packing the meat too closely, handling the meat as little as possible. When the chafing dish is hot, butter just enough to prevent sticking; toss in the balls, shake gently for 3 minutes and season with salt, pepper and butter.

EMPANADAS

Prepare cold meat as for "pasteles", adding perhaps a few capers. Enclose in a rich pastry as turn-overs and bake in a quick oven. The recipe for "Pasteles" maye be found under "Christmas Dishes." Made very small, "empanadas" are delicious served hot with cocktails.

CURRIED MEAT

Cut up left over chickens, pork or veal
½ can tomatoes
1 small onion
1 minced apple

½ teaspoonful ground ginger
1 teaspoonful curry powder
½ teaspoonful tumeric

Add water if necessary to these ingredients when cooking, to make sauce thinner. Serve with dry boiled rice.

ROPA VIEJA (OLD CLOTHES)

3 cups cooked beef
2 tablespoons butter
2 tablespoons flour
3 tomatoes

1 onion
3 green peppers
Garlic
Pepper and salt

This takes its name from the appearance of the meat which is prepared by tearing it into flakes. Heat butter, add flour, stir and simmer until well browned. Add tomatoes, an onion, chopped, green peppers chopped, a bit of garlic ground in a mortar, pepper and salt to taste, then the cooked flaked beef. Water may be added to form sufficient sauce.

CALVES BRAINS

1 pair brains
2 tablespoons butter
3 eggs

Cooked mushrooms
Pepper and salt
Parsley

Prepare a pair of brains by first soaking in cold water to draw out the blood, then trim off the membranes and fibers, drop into scalding water and allow to remain five or six minutes. Cut into dice, sauté on hot pan with butter until they whiten. Add beaten eggs, one-half teaspoonful of salt and one-fourth teaspoonful of pepper, and stir until the eggs are just set. Serve garnished with chopped parsley and cooked mushrooms.

BOILED TONGUE

Wash a tongue, put it into enough cold water to cover it; let it soak overnight. The next morning wash it, put it over the fire in enough fresh cold water to cover, and boil gently until very tender; then remove the skin, return it to the liquor it was boiled in, and let it cool there. This will make it very tender and juicy.

BEEF TONGUE WITH TOMATO SAUCE

1 tongue boiled until tender and peeled	1 carrot
1 can tomatoes	Salt and pepper
1 onion	1 tablespoon flour

Make a sauce of the above ingredients and pour over the tongue. Serve hot.

TO DRESS CHICKENS

Take fresh killed chickens, clean, cut up and scald in hot water without giving them time to cool. If chickens do not grow cold before dressing they will be tender.

CHICKEN IN CASSEROLE

2 chickens weighing 3 pounds or more each	Potatoes
Butter, pork or bacon fat	1 tablespoon lemon juice
Small onions	Salt and pepper

This dish is at its best when made with chickens weighing about three pounds or a little more. For a choice dish use two chickens, making broth of the bulky pieces in which to cook the rest of the chicken. The day before the dish is to be served, cut the chickens in pieces at the joints. Cover the carefully washed necks, backs and giblets, except the livers, with cold water and let cook till the flesh is tender. Cool the broth, skim, and it is ready for use. The pieces of chicken can be used in some other dish. Sauté the pieces of raw chicken in a little hot clarified butter, pork or bacon fat, then transfer them to a casserole. Heat the broth to the boiling point, pour it over the contents, cover close, and let cook very gently in the oven till the chicken is nearly tender. Have ready as many small parboiled onions as there are people to serve, also six or eight potato balls, cut with a French scoop, a young carrot cut in quarters, and peas, for each service. Sauté all these vegetables in the frying pan until well browned. The onions should have been boiled at least an hour, then rinsed and dried before sautéing. About fifteen minutes before serving the dish, skim off all fat from the broth; add the browned vegetables, a tablespoonful or lemon juice, salt and pepper as needed, and return the dish, covered close, to the oven. If a thicker sauce be desired, thicken the broth with flour, before adding it to the dish; skim off the fat at time of serving and a particularly velvety sauce results.

ARROZ CON POLLO No. 1
(RICE WITH CHICKEN)

1 chicken	1/3 cup capers
1/2 cup olive oil	1/2 cup olives
Parsley	Spanish peppers
3/4 pound rice	2 cloves garlic
2 teaspoons salt	

This is one of the most typical dishes in Puerto Rico.

Disjoint a chicken and cut the larger portions in fairly small pieces. Brown it in a half cup of olive oil, and chopped parsley. Now add three-fourths of a pound of rice and after it has taken on a golden color, add three cups of water and cook slowly, keeping covered so as to preserve the aroma. The rice should be cooked through but not broken open. Add two teaspoons salt, one-third cup capers and half a cup of olives cut up, garnish with Spanish peppers, and serve hot.

ARROZ CON POLLO No. 2
(RAFAELA MATIENZO)

1 chicken, 3½ to 4 pounds	2 cups rice
½ cup bacon	Capers
½ cup salt pork	Small cooking olives
¾ cup tomato sauce	Sweet red peppers
1 large onion	2 cloves garlic
Bay-leaf	

Salt and boil chicken and follow recipe for Sofrito.

SOFRITO

Bacon and salt pork, about ½ cup each cut small; put to fry; fry brown. Now add about ¾ cup tomato sauce, one large onion, one sweet pepper, chopped, bay-leaf. Cook together ten minutes.

Add Sofrito to broth, have chicken taken from bones and free from skin. Let sofrito and broth cook five minutes.

Wash about 2 cups rice and add to broth and sofrito. Cook ½ hour gently. Add a few capers and small cooking olives, then meat of chicken. Garnish with sweet red peppers.

If rice is soaked a little while in tepid water after being washed, it will be more tender, and cook in shorter time than otherwise. The ingredients of "sofrito", the flavorings, are usually pounded together in a mortar. A small wooden mortar is a needed equipment for every kitchen.

"ASOPAO"

Chicken and rice can also be cooked by stewing the chicken instead of frying it.

"Asopao" is made by adding more water so that the rice is moist instead of dry. In fact almost "soupy". Add a can of asparagus tips and one of small peas, leaving them on top of the rice without stirring, and serve very hot.

ROAST PIGEONS

Pigeons	Salt	Cloves
Butter	Red wine	Flour

Pick out the pin feathers or if there are a great many, skin the pigeons. Examine inside very carefully. Soak half an hour in cold water, to take out the blood. Boil half an hour in salted water, and take off the scum as fast as it rises. Then stuff with chicken dressing, roast for an hour basting with butter. For the dressing take the drippings, a cup of the liquor they were boiled in, a piece of butter and a little flour; put in half a glass of red wine and half a teaspoonful of cloves. Give it one boil.

GUINEA FOWL

1 guinea fowl	Salt	Toast
Lemon juice	Flour	Lemon or lime slices
Butter	Bacon	Parsley

The Spaniards found the Borinquen Indians using the guinea fowl for food, it being native to the island.

Dress, clean, lard and truss a guinea fowl. Cover with lemon juice for an hour or two. Then with salt, brush over with melted butter, dredge with flour and cover with a few pieces of bacon. Bake in a hot oven, basting several times. Arrange on platter, garnish with small pieces of toast, thin slices of lemon or lime and parsley. Wild rice or unpolished rice, boiled, and jelly should accompany this course. Guinea fowl is also nice cooked in casserole.

STUFFED TURKEY No. 1
(BEATRICE BRUNO VAZQUEZ)

1 pound butter	¼ pound almonds
1 pound pork	½ pound ham
1 bottle small olives	¼ bacon
¾ box prunes	1 pound onion
1 glass sauterne wine	Vinegar to taste
Cocktail sausages	2 hard-boiled eggs
3 green peppers	1 pound tomatoes
Capers	Worcestershire sauce

Salt, pepper, lemon

Kill the turkey a day ahead of the time it is to be used. Clean and draw. Rub it well inside and out with salt, freshly ground pepper, and lemon. Put it in ice-box to cool. Grind the pork, ham, bacon and onion. Chop the olives, capers, prunes, raisins, green pepper, sweet pepper. Cut the eggs, tomatoes and liver, heart and gizzard of the turkey (previously cooked) into pieces; salt and pepper. Put all above into a saucepan to fry with the sausages. Add the wine. Stuff the turkey with this mixture; put pieces of butter under the wings and butter the entire surface of the turkey, putting slices of onion over it. Every half hour baste it and turn it frequently while roasting.

STUFFED TURKEY No. 2
(ISABEL BECERRA)

½ pound bread	2 apples cut in pieces
¼ pound butter	1 pound nuts
½ pound liverwurst	3 eggs
½ pound beef or pork	Bacon

Put the bread to soak in enough water or milk to cover, and grind the meat and liverwurst. Add the butter and the eggs. Cook in a saucepan without browning, only to heat, and add the nuts and apples, finely chopped. Stuff the turkey with this, place strips of bacon over it and bake in the oven.

PAELLA VALENCIANA

½ cup olive oil	Tomato
1 chicken	Salt and pepper
½ pound ham	Saffron
½ pound bacon	1 cup rice
Sweet pepper	

Let olive oil heat in a casserole or iron pot, put in a chicken cut up, ham cut fine, bacon cut fine. When it browns put in small pieces of sweet pepper and tomato, enough water to cover. Add ground pepper and enough saffron to give a good color. When this cooks together a few minutes add sufficient stock or water to cook the rice. Put in a cup of well washed rice, reduce the heat and let it cook so that the rice is done but each grain separate. Salt and pepper to taste. After cooking put it aside on the hot top of the stove *á reposar*—to repose or rest, as they say in Spanish. This is for the excess liquid to dry out. This must be carefully made. After the rice is once in, no water should be added. If the liquid seems too much, increase the flame in order to reduce it. The pot should be large in proportion to the amount cooked so that the rice may be a little thick and evenly cooked.

"MONDONGO"
AÑASCO

3 pounds tripe	1 close garlic
Juice of 1 lime	1 teaspoon coriander seeds
1 calf's foot	1 slice bread
2 tablespoons butter	Milk or broth
Salt and pepper	¼ pound diced ham
1 leaf each culantro and culantrillo	¼ pound diced bacon
Oregano	1 tablespoon capers
8 or 10 blanched almonds	16 Spanish olives
Saffron	Pieces of yuca, plantain, sweet potato

Cut up tripe, squeeze a lime over it, add cold water to cover. Add a calf's foot cut in pieces, butter, salt and pepper; cook until tender. Pound in a mortar a leaf of culantro, one of culantrillo, a little oregano, 8 or 10 blenched almonds, a little saffron, garlic, coriander seeds, mix with a slice of bread soaked in broth or milk. Fry diced ham and diced bacon, add the herbs, capers and olives. Add this mixture to the pot with pieces of "yuca", plantain and sweet potato. Let simmer until done and serve from a tureen into soup plates.

SANCOCHO
(LOIZA)

2 pounds pork	Lime juice
1 onion	1 teaspoon salt
1 clove of garlic	Whole hot peppers
1 bay-leaf	Pieces yuca roots, yellow squash
Parsley	and plantain
Culantro	Corn bread or cassava

Pound sliced onion, garlic, bay-leaf and a few leaves of parsley and "culantro" in a mortar. Add lime juice to absorb the flavor, 1 teaspoon salt and a few whole hot peppers. Add this to the pork cut into pieces; stew for an hour in enough water to cover. Then put in a few pieces of "yuca" roots, yellow squash and plantain. Mash the squash to slightly thicken the stew. When done serve in soup plates with corn bread or cassava.

MOFONGO

"Chicharrón"	Salt and pepper
1 yellow plantain	Olive oil or lard
1 clove garlic	

"Chicharrón" is the skin of the pork cooked so as to fry out the lard. It is sold by the vendors in a glass box. Take all the little pieces of crisp fat and lean meat from a piece of "chicharrón", run them through the meat chopper. Fry a yellow plantain in slices. Then pound them in a mortar, alternating with the pork. Add a clove of garlic, salt and pepper. When all is mashed well put in a saucepan to heat with a little olive oil or lard.

STEWED KID No. 1

6 cloves garlic mashed in a mortar	½ pint olive oil
1½ pounds onion cut fine	3 bay-leaves
3 cans Spanish sweet red peppers	Salt
6 cans tomato sauce	2 cans peas
5 pounds small potatoes	1 bottle olives
1 bottle grape juice	Brandy to taste

Kill the kid the day before using, hang it up. Carefully take out entrails. The next day wash it with sour orange juice or lemon. Wash then in water and cut in pieces. Put together the ingredients in a kettle and place on a slow fire to cook well.

STEWED KID No. 2
(SRA. BASSÓ)

1 kid
Lemon juice
Pure olive oil
2 or 3 cloves garlic
1 bay-leaf
Olives, raisins and capers.

Small potatoes
8 to 10 whole peppers to each
    pound kid
3 or 4 cloves
1 glass wine for each pound
    kid

Kill a kid day before using, wash with lemon juice leaving it in the juice for a time. Wash with water and cut into fairly small pieces. Use pure olive oil (no lard, no ham or bacon). Mix 2 or 3 cloves of garlic, bay-leaf, whole olives, raisins and capers, small potatoes with a little water, whole pepper (8 or 10) to a pound of kid and 3 or 4 cloves. Put all together in a pottery casserole, cover with wax-paper or white paper. Put on a slow fire. Add water a little at a time until the kid is tender. Add a glass of wine for each pound of kid. This recipe is also good for chicken.

RABBIT

1 rabbit
Lemon juice
Salt
½ cup olive oil
½ cup white wine

2 cloves garlic
Few small onions
1 bay-leaf
4 whole peppers
Parsley

Make an incision down the thighs of the back legs. Turn the legs through this incision and begin to work the skin up, inside out, skinning it towards the head. Make an incision the length of the abdomen, carefully remove insides without breaking them. Clean it inside with water, then lemon juice and salt. Cut the rabbit into pieces, put them in a kettle with a half cup of olive oil, a half cup of white wine, 2 cloves of garlic, a few small onions, bay-leaf, 4 whole peppers, parsley and salt. Add a cup of water, cover the kettle by stretching a piece of white paper over and tying it down. Let cook slowly for an hour and a half.

HERBS

"Small herbs have grace."—Richard III.

VOLUMES could be written on our medical botany of which "small herbs" form such a part. Very many of the indigenous plants are to be found in Grosourdy's *Medical Botany*. "Ajonjoli", "pomarrosa", "allamanda", "algarrobo", "morivivi", the little sensitive plant, the various mints and salvias all have virtues. From many of them are made "tisanas" or syrups rich in curative principles. To primitive man trees and plants were part of his life. They live and they die, the same as a person, so he thinks they have souls like his own and treats them accordingly. Thus, in the evolution of civilized man we may account for many so-called superstitions which may be traced to beliefs in folkways the world over. Herbs have always played a great part in these beliefs, related as they are to magic, to taboos, or occultism in worship and ritual. Traces of plants worship are found in all parts of the world and in various folktales much plant-lore may be found. From earliest times plants have been used in the cure of disease so it is not such a far cry from their mystical history to scientific fact.

Perhaps our fascination in raising herbs is due to the legendary lore surrounding them. There certainly is nothing more charming than the peace and seclusion of an herb garden. The mistress of old used her garden in a practical way to grow plants to cure the sick and much time was spent in making healing ointments, washing waters and aromatic draughts, cordials, scented candles, sweet herbs for storing linens and to keep away moths. Our patchouli is one of these, which we use today; it is the root of a grass-like plant belonging to the mint family. In olden times furniture was rubbed with herbs to give a pleasant smell and floors were strewed with them, as they gave off an odor on being bruised when they were stepped on. In the very delightful book *The Conqueror,* the life of Alexander Hamilton, by Gertrude Atherton, which gives such a perfect picture of West Indian life two hundred years ago, the women polished the floors with orange skins, the oil of the skin producing a good polish.

Some of our herbs no doubt are indigenous, some must have been brought from Europe in early days of the settlement. No doubt the early settlers learned how to use the native herbs and remedies from the Borinquen Indians. We can picture the gentle Inéz, the wife of Ponce de Léon, as she moved about her garden, tenderly nursing the plants so new to her, and taking delight in their fragrance. There are many local herbs valuable for their essential oils: bay, bergamot, eucalyptus, jasmine, lemon, orange, rose, mint, ylang-ylang, are but a few of them.

Sweet smelling herbs were used in olden times for incense. In Biblical times "the burnt offering, sweet scents," were "put before the testimony in the tent of meeting." In the days when ships were far between, Pope Pius, in 1581, granted a faculty to the bishops of the West Indies permitting the substitution of native balsam, *miroxylum preiciferum,* for the balsam of India in preparation of the chrism to be used by the Roman Catholic Church in America. The "sangre del Drago," Croton Drago, one of the Euphorbiaceæ was also used. Garden thyme, a native of southern Europe is found in the market, its odor sweet and spicy. Formerly a tea made from the leaves was much esteemed as a tonic and the leaves were used to season meats, dressings and sauces. A few plants in the garden will keep a supply always on hand. Our great grandmothers put away their woolens for the summer with thyme, rosemary and cloves. The Spanish were fond of rosemary (*romero*). From an old Spanish proverb it seems to have been connected with love:

> "Who passeth by the rosemary
> Nor shall he though he live for aye."
> And dareth not to take a spraye
> For woman's love no care has he,

And in Calderon's *El Alcalde de Zalamea* the Captain sings under Isabel's window:

> "Las flores del romero,
> Niña Isabel
> Hoy son flores azules
> Y mañana seran miel."

Rosemary is much valued for its bracing aromatic odor and when steeped, is used as a lotion.

Sweet marjoram, *oregano vulgare,* is the "orégano" of the market place. It is used both fresh and dried. The small oval grey-green velvety leaf is charming in contrast with plants of brighter green. It is used like sage in flavoring. As an ornamental it cannot be overestimated. The name is said to mean "joy of the mountains," an apt name to all who love old-fashioned flowers. It is not only liked for culinary purposes but medicinally valuable as a tonic. According to a writer of an early day, marjoram was used in "sweete powders, bags, and sweete washing waters."

Originally garlic was used only for medicine, the allyl sulphide it contains is a nerve stimulant. In ancient times garlic was taken by Greek and Roman soldiers as a part of their rations for it was believed that it incited them to great courage and allayed fatigue.

Rue, *ruda cabruna,* makes a beautiful appearance in a garden with its lacy leaves of jade-green. The flavor is pungent. Used in strewing in medieval times, it was supposed to ward off contagion. Rue is one of the few herbs that appear in heraldry, and sprigs of rue figure in the Collar of the Order of the Thistle. The herb is said to have been potent against intermeddling of fairies. According to a story, a man held captive by fairy spirits noted their avoidance of rue, and escaped by grasping handfuls of the plant. Shakespeare speaks of it as a "sweet herbe of grace," and it is said sprays of it were used with which to sprinkle holy water, hence the reference. Rue does well in soil possessing lime and is at its best in full sunlight.

Albaranilla is a blue flowered onion. The root is mashed in a mortar and used to flavor soups and meats.

Berros, (Rorippa nasturticion) water cress, is usually in market. It grows in mountain streams and is delicious in sandwiches and salads. It is rich in iron.

Capsicum, (Capsicum annuum) is the pimiento, chili of commerce. The fruits of *Capsicum frutescens,* are used in the preparation of cayenne pepper.

Aji is the dwarf red pepper, but there are many varieties in market; the small yellow round pepper, which also comes green, and the tiny very red pepper. There are the large pointed red and green peppers and the sweet peppers, that have distinct flavor apart from their hot quality. Pound them in a mortar and add to soups and meats. Pepper sauce is made by crushing six chili peppers in a mortar adding juice of a lime as you crush, with a bit of salt. This is served at table to put on beans and rice.

Culantro, (coriamdrum sativum) is the coriander of the north. It has young tender plants with long lobed serrated leaves. Crushed in a mortar it is agreeable for the pungent flavor it gives and is especially good in stews.

Basil brings to mind Keats' story of Isabella and her pot of basil. To my mind there is nothing in the way of herbs that surpasses the sweet basils, "albahaca" *(Ocinum basilicum* and *Ocinum cimmarona-cea).* The shining-leaved perky little sprays soon grow into woody eighteen-inch plants that not only are ornamental but give forth a pungent fragrance; added to bouquets they keep the water in vases fresh and untainted as well as providing a delicate green to accompany flowers. The green-leaved basil has white flowers while the *morada,* whose leaves are lined with purple, has lavender flowers. Both are added to soups, stews, sauces, and are especially good added to tomato dishes. The leaves are charming to put in finger bowls. An old English writer said of basil; "The Physicall properties are to procure a cheerful and merry heart."

Use parsley garnish with chops and fish, cress with meats, and mint with lamb. Provide garnishes that can be eaten. A sprig of parsley is said to be an excellent liver tonic. Slices of lime or lemon should be served with fish and lime leaves make a decorative border for fish or cold meats.

The mints belong to one of the largest families of herbs. Penny-royal, *poleo, Mentha pulegium,* is perhaps the smallest of the mints. Its botanical name comes from the fact that it was used to rid rooms of fleas, according to Pliny. The herb was much used to flavor stuffings in olden times. It is also much used medicinally.

Sándalo, or bergamot mint *(mestha odorata)* is a smooth-leaved variety of mint very much relied upon as a remedy for indigestion by country people. The local variety is not related to the northern bergamot which belongs to the balm family but the odor is somewhat similar.

The *yerbabuena*—peppermint *(Mentha)*—is to be found always in market. It is easily grown but in a garden it soon overruns all else. In some parts of the island it has escaped from gardens and grows wild. It is used in country districts to cure colic, cholera morbus, and in lotions and baths. Tea made from the leaves is good to break up a cold. Planted around a bird-bath it is lovely, or in a corner, where abandoned, it soon occupies all space available. The leaves candied are fine for iced-tea or to accompany hot tea. Mint has become one of our most popular flavors and can be used in numerous combinations of food and drink. Every one knows how essential the mint flavor is to lamb. Mint sauce and mint jelly may be preserved and kept for months by the following recipes:

MINT SAUCE

Pick over and wash enough mint leaves to fill a large pan; for every cup of leaves, allow one cup of vinegar, one cup of water, one and a half cups of sugar and a pinch of salt. Extract the juices by pounding the leaves to a pulp; then add the above and boil until the mixture becomes like thick syrup. Pour into jelly glasses and cover with paraffin.

MINT JELLY

½ package gelatine   Green vegetable coloring
Mint sauce made as above   Salt
Juice of 1 lemon

Dissolve gelatin in half cup of cold water; add one cup mint sauce, the juice of a lemon, salt, and one pint of boiling water. To make a brighter green use a few drops of green vegetable coloring. Strain into jelly glasses and cover with paraffin.

BOUQUET OF HERBS FOR SOUP

Six small parsley stalks, one branch celery, one blade of bay-leaf, one sprig thyme. Place two cloves in the center of parsley to prevent them falling out of bouquet when cooking; fold all well together and tie with a string. This makes a good flavoring for soups.

Fascinating books have been written on the subject of herbs and one may find much material in Puerto Rico, but the above mentioned are only a few of our most common and well-known herbs.

YAUTIA

VEGETABLES

"Look into the seeds of time, and say which grain will grow and which will not."

ALL vegetables should be well picked over and washed. A very little salt should always be thrown into the water in which they are boiled. They should never for a moment be allowed to stop boiling or simmering till they are thoroughly done. Every sort of vegetable should be cooked till tender, since if the least hard or underdone they are both unpalatable and unwholesome. The practice of putting saleratus in the pot to improve the color of green vegetables should be strictly forbidden, as it destroys the flavor, and either renders them flat and insipid or communicates a very disagreeable taste of its own. Every sort of culinary vegetable is infinitely best when fresh from the garden, and gathered as short a time as possible before it is cooked. All juicy and green vegetables should be very fresh and succulent, and are best just before flowering, as also are the sweet herbs called pot herbs. Roots and tubers should be full and fresh colored; if withered they are inferior. Green vegetables should not be bought in larger quantities than can be used while they are still fresh; they should be sprinkled with water and laid in a cool, dark place. After cooking drain carefully before sending to table. Have a small brush for cleaning vegetables and two small sharp knives in your kitchen. Save the water in which vegetables have been boiled for soups or stews, or nicely flavored, it may be served as an appetizer at the beginning of a meal.

ARRACACHA, APIO OR CELERY PLANT

An early writer said of this vegetable, "The production of this island which excels all others is the root very like turnips of a tapering shape except that they grow somewhat larger like the pumpkin. When eaten raw, as in salads, they have the taste of parsnips; when roasted, that of chestnuts; when sodden with pork, that of squashes; when sprinkled with juice of almonds nothing can taste more delicious, or is eaten with greater avidity. These esculents afford an excellent material for the exercise of the culinary art, and are well adapted for eating houses and taverns."

The *arracacha* is one of the most delicious tubers, and one too little known although it can nearly always be found in market. It is said that the Italians gave it the name of *apio* from the resemblance of its flavor to that of celery. Rich in a starch which is easily digested, it is valuable as a food for convalescents. Scrape the roots and cut into dice, put on to boil. When soft drain off the water and dress with salt, pepper and butter.

FRIED ARRACACHA

Cut into thin slices, parboil, then drain and brown in butter.

BUÑUELOS DE APIO

Clean the roots, then grate them. Flavor with butter, pepper and salt, press into croquettes, roll in flour and drop into hot fat until brown.

APIO SOUFFLÉ

1 cup grated apio	2 tablespoons flour
½ cup milk	Beaten whites of three eggs
¼ cup sugar	

Fold stiffly beaten egg-whites into the mixture. Bake the same as any soufflé and serve with a cream sauce.

APIO OR ARRACACHA SOUP

Cook the root in salted water, pass through a sieve. Heat a quart of milk, thicken it with a tablespoon of butter rubbed into ¾ cup of flour, add 2 cups of the strained arracacha, ¼ teaspoon pepper, 1 teaspoon salt. In each soup-plate put a teaspoonful minced parsley and a dash of nutmeg.

Potatoes, yam, *yautia*, squash, yuca, may all be used in the same way.

ARROWROOT

Arrowroot is botanically known as *maranta arundinacea*, of the *marantaceae* family. It is an herbaceous plant with tubers from which arrowroot is extracted. Its name comes on account of the property it has of counteracting the poison which was put on their arrow tips by the Indians. It is also used to cure insect bites. The plant is easily grown and indigenous to many tropical countries. In China it is very generally used in cookery where it is called the water chestnut. In St. Vincent and other islands of the West Indies the tubers are cultivated on a large scale to take out the starch which is sold in commerce. The Spaniards found the Indians using them here as food, they called them *llerenes*. *Llerenes* or *lerenes* have a thin skin, a somewhat transparent interior which is always crisp even when cooked.

Boiled in salted water, then peeled, they are delicious. They may be creamed, or served boiled and cold in a salad.

LERENES SALAD

Boil and peel "lerenes"; cut them fine. Rub a salad bowl with a clove of garlic, add lettuce or cress and marinate well with French dressing.

SWEET POTATO, *Ipomoea Batata, Batata*

Some writers have claimed that the word *batata* is of Malayan origin, and that the sweet potato is therefore of Asiatic origin. However it seems that it was cultivated by the aborigines in tropical America before the coming of the Spaniards.

There are many varieties of the sweet potato, judging from the varieties of leaf forms.

The sweet potato is mentioned by a visitor in 1519, who found it in use among the Indians as an article of food. The plant was carried to Spain, from thence it spread over Europe and was common there before the so-called Irish potato was known. Doctor Pavi says "The tubers were imported into England by way of Spain, and sold as a delicacy before the potato was known, and it forms the article referred to when the name is mentioned by English writers previous to the middle of the 17th century."

They have many varieties, the flowers and tubers varying from pure white to dark purple. Many species are native to the West Indies and constitute an important food. They are eaten boiled, baked, fried or mashed like potatoes. Any of these tubers may be used in a recipe for potatoes; as a rule they require a little more milk in their preparation for they are all a little less moist than the potato.

BAKED SWEET POTATOES No. 1

Boil six sweet potatoes until tender, peel and slice; spread in a flat pan, throw over them a cup of sugar and dot generously with butter. Use at least half cup butter. Bake until well browned.

BAKED SWEET POTATOES No. 2

Select those of uniform size, wash clean, cutting out any imperfect spots, wipe dry, put into a moderately hot oven, and bake about one hour, or until the largest will yield to gentle pressure between the fingers. Serve at once without peeling. Small potatoes are best steamed, since if baked, the skins will take up nearly the whole potato.

BROWNED SWEET POTATOES

Slice cold cooked sweet potatoes evenly, place on slightly oiled tins in a hot oven, and brown.

SWEET POTATO CROQUETTES

2 eggs
Bread-crumbs
Boiled sweet potatoes to make a pint

½ cupful hot milk
2 generous tablespoonfuls butter
1 teaspoonful salt

When the potatoes have been mashed smooth and light, beat into them the hot milk and then the salt and butter, next beat one egg until light and beat this into the mixture which should now be shaped into eight croquettes. Beat the second egg in a soup plate; cover the croquettes with the egg and roll them in the bread-crumbs. Fry till they turn a rich brown. Serve at once.

SWEET POTATO PUFF

2 cups of cold mashed sweet potatoes
2 tablespoons melted butter
2 eggs whipped very light

1 cup of milk
Salt to taste

Beat potatoes and butter to a cream, beat ingredients very well together and pour into a deep dish and bake in a hot oven until it is nicely browned.

CANDIED SWEET POTATOES

Pare and parboil half dozen sweet potatoes, cut in halves, lengthwise. After ten minutes boiling, drain and lay in a baking dish. Spread thick with butter, sprinkle with brown or maple sugar, and, if desired, a little powdered cinnamon; add a few spoonfuls of hot water and bake until tender, basting often with the sauce in the pan.

SWEET POTATO PIE

1 pound grated potatoes
¾ pound of sugar
½ cupful cream

½ pound butter
4 eggs

Proceed as in making squash pie.

DIFFERENT WAYS
OF COOKING SWEET POTATOES

(1) Boil until almost cooked, then peel and slice. Sprinkle with brown sugar and fry in hot water. (2) Peel and slice raw. Soak a bit in iced-water then fry in hot lard. (3) Boil and peel, mash with butter. Cover with brown sugar in a baking dish and bake in the oven. (4) Peel and put around under a roast of meat and cook at the same time. They will brown over and have a delicious flavor.

STRING BEANS No. 1

Wash and string the beans, cutting them diagonally across. Boil in salted water until tender with a piece of bacon. Add salt and pepper to taste.

STRING BEANS No. 2

Prepare as above, make a cream sauce with butter and flour, adding cream or milk, mix in the beans. Serve very hot.

FRESH LIMA BEANS
Habas

Put a quart of shelled lima beans over the fire, in sufficient boiling water to cover them, with a tablespoonful of salt, and boil them for about twenty minutes, or until they are tender; then drain them, add to them enough milk to cover them, a tablespoonful of butter, and a palatable seasoning of salt and white pepper; heat them quickly, and serve them hot.

FRIJOLES

Frijoles are delicious picked green and tender like string beans. Boil and serve with butter or in white sauce.

WHITE BEAN PUDDING

Boil the beans until soft, strain and add salt and pepper; fry bacon and an onion until brown and mix with the beans. Put in a greased pan and bake, adding a little butter from time to time.

RED BEANS

1 cup red beans	½ cup tomatoes
Bacon and salt pork	Sweet peppers
1 chopped onion	Salt and pepper

Soak beans overnight in water. Put on to stew gently. Take some bacon and salt pork, cut into small pieces and fry. Add a chopped onion and fry brown, then add tomatoes, salt and pepper and let this mixture cook slowly. When the beans are soft, add this mixture to them, cover and let simmer. Just before serving add sweet peppers which have had the seeds and skin removed. If the gravy seems thin it may be thickened with flour, or a little mashed squash. Serve over dry boiled rice. Rice-and-beans is almost a national dish, served daily in most homes in Puerto Rico.

HOPPING JOHN

One cup of dried cow peas (black-eyed peas) soaked in water to cover overnight. Boil with a piece of bacon. When peas are done, drain. Prepare a *sofrito* by frying small pieces of ham, a small onion cut up, a tomato, a tablespoon minced sweet pepper, salt and pepper. Skim off the grease from water peas have cooked in, add the *sofrito* to the peas and stir together with a cupful of rice which has been cooked separately. If it seems too wet, set in oven to dry out. Serve with fried sausage or bacon.

BREADFRUIT

The well known breadfruit *(Artocarpus incisa)* is one of the most beautiful of tropical trees and has provided food for ages for man, having been one of the trees to establish itself in the cretaceous age. Around it are woven tales of romance and adventure. It will be recalled that it was in order to obtain seeds of this tree for planting in the West Indies that the English Admiral Captain Bligh went through harrowing adventures. He had accompanied Captain Cook as sailing master on the *Resolution,* when they discovered this tree in the South Sea islands. So determined was he to transplant the tree he gained the nickname of "Breadfruit Bligh". In 1787 he undertook the trip again to secure the seeds, on the ship *Bounty* when the mutiny broke out which cast him adrift in an open boat. Byron wrote of this incident in *Island* and it became the subject of *Mutiny on the Bounty* by Nordoff and Hall. On a third voyage he successfully accomplished the introduction of 1,000 plants of the breadfruit into the West Indies.

Many varieties of the tree are cultivated, one bears a fruit containing seeds not unlike chestnuts. In others the seeds are abortive and the fruit is cooked as a vegetable. Baked, the fruit is delicious. As it ripens gradually and the tree bears throughout the year, it constantly affords a food supply. Sliced and dried in the sun it can be grated or ground into flour. It is used in the East as a foundation for curries.

BAKED BREADFRUIT

Peel a breadfruit and slice in small thin slices. Put in a buttered baking dish with salt and pepper to season. Pour on milk to cover and bake in a moderate oven.

BREADFRUIT CREAMED

Boil, cutting fruit into small cubes; serve with a cream made with one tablespoon of butter and one of flour, stirred into half pint of boiling milk.

BREADFRUIT CROQUETTES

Boil breadfruit in salt water until tender, mash, season, and add a good chunk of butter, the yolk of an egg, roll in flour and fry.

BREADFRUIT NUTS

Breadfruit nuts should be boiled, skinned and served hot with butter and salt. Use them in place of bread in turkey stuffing.

BREADFRUIT NUT SALAD

Two cups breadfruit nuts cut up, two cups celery finely cut, serve on lettuce with French dressing and garnish with stuffed olives.

CHAYOTE

The chayote is a cucurbit, native of the West Indies. It is propagated by planting the whole ripe fruit containing the seeds. It grows into a vine and is said to bear 300 to 500 fruits in a season. It is not unlike a squash in flavor but much more delicate.

A fruit is a direct product of a flower, thus many vegetables are in truth a fruit, such as squash, chayote, pumpkin, papaya, cucumber, etc. The chayote *(sechium edule)* has about twelve varieties, they vary in size and color ranging from dark green to palest ivory.

MASHED CHAYOTES

Cut in quarters, boil in the skin, then peel. Season well and mash. Serve as mashed squash.

SCALLOPED CHAYOTES

Cut chayotes in half and boil until tender, scoop out center, mix with the yolk of an egg, season well, return to the shells, sprinkle with cracker-crumbs and grated cheese and brown.

STUFFED CHAYOTES

Cut chayotes in half and boil until tender, scoop out center, mix with chopped meat, season well and return to the shells, sprinkle with bread-crumbs and bake until brown.

FRIED CHAYOTES

Peel chayotes and boil in salt and water until a fork will enter readily. Take out of the water, cut into slices, dip into egg and cracker-crumbs and fry.

FRICASSEE OF CHAYOTES

Peel and boil chayotes until tender, season and fry in butter, as you hash brown potatoes. Before serving scramble two eggs over them.

CHAYOTE CREAMED

Peel and cut into cubes and boil tender. Drain off water and add sufficient cream diluted with water, season with salt, pepper and butter. Crack the nut of chayote, remove the kernel and chop it to use as a garnish or to scatter over the cooked chayote. It gives an added flavor and is nourishing.

BORONIA DE CHAYOTES

3 chayotes	Salt and pepper	1 garlic clove
½ cup pork	1 onion	1 leaf culantro
½ cup ham	1 tomato	¼ teaspoon paprika
3 eggs	½ green pepper	

Boil three chayotes, take from peel and cut into small pieces. Take half a cup each of pork meat and ham, run through a grinder and heat in a casserole. Add an onion, a tomato, ½ of a green pepper, a garlic clove, a leaf of culantro, a teaspoon of salt, ¼ teaspoon paprika and a dash of pepper, all chopped and mixed together, to the meat. Add half a cup water and let cook slowly a few minutes. Then add the chayote and cook five minutes more, and at the last moment add three beaten eggs. Put out gas and do not cook after adding the eggs for the heat will cook them sufficiently. Serve hot as the principal luncheon dish.

CHAYOTE SALAD

Boil chayotes, cut up, using the meat of the nut also. Sprinkle with celery seed and serve upon lettuce with boiled dressing. Onions may also be combined with chayote.

CORN

"And before the summer ended
Stood the maize in all its beauty,
With its shining robes about it,
And its long, soft, flowing tresses;
And in rapture Hiawatha
Cried aloud, 'It is Mondamin
Yes, the friend of man, Mondamin.' "

Corn, in Europe, meant any grain or cereal, hence the application of that word to maize, which is an Indian word.

Probably no cereal or vegetable is so common to all parts of America as is corn, or has nourished so many peoples of the world. Its cultivation and growth and harvest are embodied in all the folklore of the Indians of the Western Hemisphere and in parts of the old world as well. Like sugar, corn is a member of the grass family.

GREEN CORN ON THE EAR

Select a dozen, more or less, of nice young ears, free them from every particle of silk, and throw them into boiling water with a tablespoonful of salt. If very young, fifteen minutes will cook them. As the corn grows older, it will require more time. Serve hot, with butter and salt.

FRIED CORN

Cut the corn off the ear, fry in butter, add salt and pepper.

STEWED CORN PULP

Take six ears of green corn or enough to make a pint of raw pulp; with a sharp knife cut a thin shaving from each row of kernels or score each kernel, and with the back of the knife scrape out the pulp, taking care to leave the hulls on the cob. Heat a cup and a half of rich milk—part cream—to boiling, add the corn, cook twenty or thirty minutes; season with salt and a teaspoonful of sugar if desired.

HUMITAS

Cut the corn from ½ dozen roasting ears, put through a meat chopper, press out the juice, season with salt, tablespoon of sugar, mix in one egg (unbeaten). Place a couple of spoonfuls of the mixture in two or three of the corn husks, fold and tie securely with a strip of the husk. Boil twenty minutes, serve in the husk as taken from the kettle.

CORN OYSTERS

1 can corn	½ cup flour
2 eggs	½ teaspoon salt
½ cup milk	2 teaspoons baking powder

Put corn through meat chopper, mix with other ingredients and fry as pancakes.

CORN PUDDING

1 tablespoon butter	1 cup milk
1 can corn	½ teaspoon salt
2 eggs	

Beat yolks and whites of eggs separately. Mix all ingredients adding stiff egg-whites last. Bake in quick oven and serve as a vegetable.

CUCUMBERS

FRIED CUCUMBERS No. 1

Pare cucumbers, and cut lengthwise in very thick slices; wipe them dry with a cloth; sprinkle with salt and pepper, dredge with flour, and fry in lard and butter, a tablespoon of each, mixed. Brown both sides; serve warm.

STEWED CUCUMBERS WITH ORANGE SAUCE

Cucumbers	Salt and pepper
2 tablespoons butter	Grated orange peel
1 tablespoon flour	Slices of toast
1 cup orange juice	

Cut cucumbers into quarters and boil for twenty minutes in salted water; drain and lay on toast and cover with the following sauce: Melt two table-spoonfuls of butter, add one tablespoonful of flour and one cupful of strained orange juice; stir until smooth and add salt, pepper and one salt-spoonful of grated orange peel. This is easily borne by those who cannot eat raw cucumbers.

STEWED CUCUMBERS FOR GARNISHING

Peel and slice two large cucumbers; sprinkle them with salt, pepper, add one tablespoon of vinegar; add one small slice onion; let stand for one hour, drain off the liquid, put all in a pan; cook for twenty minutes; drain through fine sieve or cheese-cloth, and use for garnishing purposes.

EGGPLANT WITH DRESSING

1 eggplant	1 small onion
1 cup chopped chicken or any meat	2 tablespoons bread-crumbs
1 tablespoon butter	Salt and pepper

Cut the eggplant in two; take out all the inside and put it in a pan with a cupful of chopped chicken, veal or any meat you wish (ham is also good); cover with water and boil until tender; drain, add one tablespoonful of butter, a small onion chopped fine, salt and pepper, and about two tablespoonfuls of bread-crumbs; mix well together and fill each half of the shell, put a little butter on each, and bake fifteen or twenty minutes.

EGGPLANT FRIED IN BUTTER

Peel and slice the egg-plant, let it lie in salt for an hour, and then roll the slices in dry flour seasoned with salt and pepper; put a large pan over the fire with enough butter to cover the bottom to the depth of half inch thick when melted; when the butter is smoking hot, put in the eggplant, fry it brown on both sides, and serve it hot.

BROILED EGGPLANT

Peel and slice a medium-sized eggplant; place the slices in a dish; season them with salt and pepper; pour over them a tablespoonful of sweet oil; broil them for five minutes on each side. Remove them from the fire, place them in a hot dish, spread four ounces of *maitre d'hotel* butter over them, and serve.

EGGPLANT PARBOILED

Parboil eggplant, cut in half and scrape out the soft part which you put in a bowl with some chopped meat and bread-crumbs. Season with salt, pepper, onions, parsley and a little ham or tongue. Put all into frying-pan a few moments, then fill eggplant shells, put bread-crumbs on top and brown in the oven.

STUFFED EGGPLANT

Cut in two and boil, scrape out the inside, and then mash as you would potatoes; add a little pepper, salt and some kind of chopped meat. Fill the shells with this mixture, sprinkle with bread-crumbs and brown.

GANDULES OR PIGEON-PEAS

The pigeon pea or *gandule* is also called Puerto Rican pea on account of its wide use as food. It becomes a shrub and grown as a hedge makes a wind-break, and also is useful as a shade for poultry. It is said the *gandule* is the same plant as the true lentils. The astronomer who ground a piece of glass until it was thin at the edge, thick in the middle, like the familiar lentil that thickened his soup, called his new invention a "lens", or "lentil". An ancient writer said, "Beans are my food, but lentils are my life". Gandules are cooked in exactly the same way as "beans and rice".

GANDULES STEWED

1 small piece of ham	2 tomatoes
2 small onions	1½ cups gandules

Chop onions fine and fry, add gandules which have been soaked overnight and parboiled, the tomatoes and ham, cover and boil. When tender add a little mashed squash.

GARBANZO

The Chick Pea *(Cicer Arietinum)*, a native of India, is commonly called *garbanzos*. It may be stewed or made into soup exactly like the dried bean.

COCIDO ESPAÑOL

3 cups garbanzos (chick peas)	1 clove
½ pound salt pork, cut fine	6 whole peppers
1 pound lean ham	2 cloves garlic
¼ pound sausage	1 cabbage
12 potatoes	Cassava meal or flour
1 onion	

Soak *garbanzos* (chick peas) overnight in water. Parboil in the morning in one quart of water. Add salt pork cut up fine, lean ham, sausage, onion, clove, peppers, garlic. Cabbage is cut up and laid over, last of all. Cover well and let stew slowly two hours or more. Thicken the broth by adding cassava meal or flour paste. Add potatoes and let cook again until the potatoes are done. It is best served in a soup plate. With a green salad to accompany it, you have a complete well-balanced meal.

OKRA HIBISCUS OR QUINGOMBO
(Abelmoschus Esculentus)

De Brazzo, the great explorer, said that in his expeditions into Africa, whenever they stopped for a few months, the first thing they planted was Okra Hibiscus, because they regarded that vegetable as most wholesome and nutritious. The cylindrical variety is the most delicate and should be picked when very tender. Cooked in any way it may be served with hot dry boiled rice.

Okra is a close relative to the hollyhock; examine its cuplike blossom and you will see its resemblance, and to the hibiscus and cotton. It was once a weed in the Congo and is believed to have been carried from Africa to the West Indies in slave boats.

It grows in the form of pods, and is of the gelatinous character, it is much used for soup, and is also pickled.

OKRA BOILED

Put the young and tender pods of long white okra in salted boiling water in granite, porcelain, or tin-lined saucepan, as contact with iron will discolor it; boil fifteen minutes; remove the stems, and serve the pods with butter; or pepper, salt and vinegar if preferred.

Okra may be added to stews, or is good in combination with rice. Serve it also as a salad, on lettuce with French dressing.

OKRA WITH BUTTER

Gather young pods of okra, wash them clean and put them in a pan with a little water, salt and pepper. Stew until tender and serve with melted butter.

OKRA WITH TOMATOES

Equal quantities of okra and tomatoes put into a saucepan, without water, with a lump of butter, an onion chopped fine, some pepper and salt, and stew one hour.

WEST INDIAN OKRA GUMBO

1 fat chicken	2 pods red pepper
1 tablespoon flour	Okra in quantity wanted
1 tablespoon pure lard	½ can tomatoes
1 onion	Salt
1 slice ham	2 cloves garlic

Stir together in a saucepan flour and lard. Chop an onion and put in.

Cut up a fat chicken into small pieces and put in. Stir until the chicken is nearly done. When well-browned, add ham cut up small; red pepper, and salt to taste. Add a quart of boiling water and leave to simmer on the stove for two hours. Slice the okra, put in another pan with a little water and simmer fifteen minutes, stirring all the time. Add tomatoes to this and cook uncovered for about an hour. When the gumbo has cooked two hours let it cool, then skim. Put it back on the fire, add the cooked okra and tomatoes and let it cook again until the okra is thoroughly done. Serve hot and with it serve dry boiled rice.

PALMILLO

Palmillo is the tender leaf bud cut from the heart of the palm tree; it is served as a vegetable or salad.

BOILED PALM

Cut the palmillo fine and boil in salted water. It may be served drained from the water and with a butter sauce poured over it.

CREAMED PALM

Boil palm in enough water to cover. Then drain off this water and prepare a white sauce. Pour sauce over palm and reheat.

PEPPERS

Sweet peppers were among the vegetables found by Columbus in the New World 400 years ago. Now they are grown in many parts of the world.

GREEN PEPPERS, SAUTÉ

Slice green peppers, remove the pungent seeds. Heat two tablespoonfuls olive oil, add the peppers and cook until tender and brown. Season with salt and serve with cold meats or steak.

STUFFED PEPPERS

Parboil in water and a little salt about ten minutes; cut in halves and take out seed and stuff with chopped meat, rice or creamed carrots; dip in egg and brown.

PILAU OF GREEN PEPPERS

Cut green peppers lengthwise, remove the seeds with care. Fill the halves with boiled rice, into which there has been stirred a tablespoonful of melted butter for a cupful of the boiled rice, and two tablespoons of grated cheese. Salt to taste. Mound the rice smooth and high and after the pilau has cooked ten minutes in a covered pan, brown lightly. Serve hot.

GREEN PEPPER SALAD

Boil the peppers, remove skin and seeds. Serve on lettuce with French or boiled dressing.

SCALLOPED GREEN PEPPERS AND HAM

Cut each pepper lengthwise into quarters and remove the seeds carefully; lay in iced-water for fifteen minutes, then drain and cut each quarter in half. Butter a pudding dish and put in the bottom of each a layer of minced ham, on top of this a layer of cut peppers. Sprinkle thickly with fine crumbs and moisten all thoroughly with seasoned stock. Then put in more ham and another layer of peppers and crumbs, liberally dotted with bits of butter and sprinkled with salt. Bake, covered, in a good oven for half an hour, then uncover and cook ten minutes longer.

RICE

The rice grown in Puerto Rico is an upland rice. It provides a diet rich in mineral salts, since it is possible to secure the rice unpolished. It should be more widely grown and partaken of. The Borinquen Indians planted three rows of rice and then one of corn.

PLAIN BOILED RICE

Take a cup of best rice, wash three times in cold water until the water is clear. The fourth time wash in hot water, put in a saucepan with enough water to cover it, salt and cover closely. Let it boil five or ten minutes. Test it with your fingers. If done, pour off water, add a quarter cupful of cold water, cover closely and set awhile on the stove to soak. If you fear its clinging to the saucepan stir with a fork, never with a spoon. Your rice will soak and dry beautifully.

BROWN RICE

Wash the rice well and dry it. Put a piece of fat into a frying-pan, when hot, fry a chopped onion and a tomato. Drop the rice into this, let it brown and cover it with stock or water. Do not stir but let it simmer until it absorbs the liquid. It may have cooked chicken, red peppers and hard-boiled eggs added and grated cheese put on top.

RICE SOUP

⅔ cup almonds pounded in a mortar with 6 bitter almonds
½ teaspoon salt   1 small onion
3 stalks celery   1 tablespoon butter

Cook together with one cup rice, in enough water to stew. Put it through a sieve and add 3 cups milk. Let boil up once and serve.

Peanuts, onion, celery, asparagus, carrot and squash may all be used in the same recipe with rice as the foundation.

RICE GUISADO

1 pound meat, fish, or lobster   ¼ pound sausages
2 onions   1 cup rice
1 large tablespoon sweet lard   1 bay-leaf
Salt and pepper   2 cloves garlic
Soup stock   1 tablespoon minced parsley
1 pound ham   Culantrillo

This is a characteristic dish with its basis one pound of either fish, lobster or any kind of meat, pork being a favorite. Cut the fish or meat into pieces about an inch square and mix with finely chopped onions. Put a large tablespoon of sweet lard into a frying-pan. When hot add the chopped pork with the onions and let them brown, cook for five minutes stirring them, add the same amount of ham as you have pork, and the sausages. Then add a bay-leaf, two cloves garlic, a tablespoon minced parsley, a bit of culantrillo, a teaspoon salt, and brown a few minutes longer. Add two quarts of water or soup stock, let cook ten minutes; then put in a cup of rice washed and dried. Season with salt and red pepper. Cook until rice is tender.

ITALIAN RICE

1 cup freshly cooked rice   1 cup grated cheese
1 tablespoon butter   1 pinch annatto
1 tablespoon flour

Have a cup freshly cooked rice; take one tablespoon butter and one of flour rubbed together in a saucepan, add a cupful grated cheese and 1½ cups of hot water and a pinch of annatto. Stir rapidly and when perfectly smooth pour this mixture over the rice spread on a shallow dish. Sprinkle with grated cheese and serve hot.

RICE CURRY

1 can tomatoes   1 tablespoon butter
6 tablespoons rice   1 saltspoon curry powder
1 onion   White pepper.

Put butter in a saucepan, grate into it the onion, add the liquor of the tomatoes, rice and seasoning. Simmer for about an hour on a low fire.

SPANISH FRIED RICE

Brown a half cup of rice in drippings, add one onion, one tomato and a little garlic. Cover with hot water, season with salt and cayenne pepper. Let rice cook perfectly, adding water as needed, but do not stir.

RICE TORTILLAS

Make a dough of one cup flour, one cup ground rice, one-half cup milk, one tablespoon butter, a little salt. Knead it thoroughly, take pieces in the hand and form into round, very thin cakes. Bake on a griddle until brown.

RICE FRITTERS

Bananas	1 egg
1 cup rice flour	½ teaspoon salt
½ cup wheat flour	1½ teaspoons baking powder
1 cup milk	

Beat the flour, half the milk, the egg yolk, salt and baking powder. Beat well with an over and over motion, add lastly the beaten white of the egg. Take up a spoonful, insert into it six slices of banana cut across, close the incision, drop into hot lard and fry to a delicate brown.

Any fruit may be used instead of the banana. The fritter may be eaten with sugar and cream, brown sugar syrup, or any fruit sauce.

BAKED SQUASH

Cut a thick squash into pieces and put into a pan with a cup of water. Cover the top of each piece with a strip of bacon, bake an hour in a hot oven. Green papayas *(lechosas)* may be cooked in the same way as squash.

SQUASH BAKED WITH CREAM

Select a ripe, knotty hubbard. Cut in halves and scoop the seeds out of one of the halves. Place on a pie tin and bake in a moderate oven. When done remove from oven and scoop the pulp from the shell into an aluminum saucepan. Return to stove and add half cup of good, sweet cream, or in lieu of that, a good-sized lump of butter and scant half-cup of milk. Season with salt. Let it cook up; stir well and serve on warm dishes. This will serve four.

STEWED SQUASH WITH TOAST

Cut squash into pieces, and stew until tender in as little water as possible. Put in colander, and let drain thoroughly, return it to the stove; add two tablespoonfuls of butter, salt and pepper to taste. Serve on toast.

SUMMER SQUASH

Peel a squash, cut it in small pieces, and boil it in salted boiling water until it is tender; drain it, put it into a clean towel and wring out all the water; put it again into saucepan over the fire, with two heaping tablespoonfuls of butter and a palatable seasoning of salt and pepper; stir it over the fire until it is hot, and serve it.

YAM, "ÑAME"

The yam, or *ñame*, belongs to a distinct botanical family, the *Dioscoreaceæ*, related to smilax and to the lily, but not to the sweet potato, as might be expected, which is of the *Ipomea* family. There are many varieties of the yam—white, yellow and red, some of better qualities than others. It grows to a large size, bearing as much as twenty pounds to a plant, and of course it is valuable as a cheap and nourishing food. Properly packed, yams may be shipped to New York and interior points of the United States.

Any recipe calling for potato may be used in preparing yams. The yam is one of our most delicious and nourishing vegetables.

Ñames, yautia, lerenes, mani, and *batatas* were growning here when the Spaniards came, and are still called by their Indian names.

Aborigines of Puerto Rico by Fewkes, says: "Some islanders of the West Indies lived wholly on *casabi* (cassava) but they had several other plants, some of which were adopted later on by civilized races. Among the latter are roots called *ages* and *batata* (sweet potato), five varieties of which are mentioned. The Indians of Haiti also cultivated *mani* (peanuts) and *yautia, (taro)* the leaves and roots of which they ate, and another plant, *axi,* was known and cultivated throughout the island. They likewise raised for food such plants as *lerenes,* and pineapples of different kind called *yayama, boniama* and *yayagua.* The fruits, *anon, guanabana, cauallos* and *mamey,* all of which have aboriginal names, were eaten and prized. It would be an important contribution to our knowledge of the diet of the aboriginal West Indians to consider food plants mentioned by the early historians, for the islanders utilized many plants that would have an economic value if added to the diet of civilized people of the Tropics."

Yams vary so in size and are so enormous that measurements in cups must be followed. The "negro yam", *Dioscorea alata,* is a choice variety of the white yams. The yellow yam is also a good table kind, sweet and wholesome.

BAKED YAM

½ cup cream or evaporated milk	2 whites of eggs
1 large yam	Salt and pepper
1 tablespoon butter	

Select a large, smooth yam, scrub it with a brush, and place in a dripping-pan. Bake in a hot oven until soft (or it may be boiled instead), then make an incision, remove the yam, leaving the skin. Mash the yam, add cream (or evaporated milk), butter, ½ teaspoon pepper, a teaspoon of salt, and whites of two eggs beaten. These proportions are for a yam that will serve four persons. Mix well and return to the shell, dot with butter, return to a hot oven to brown slightly.

BOILED YAM

Cut yam into pieces of equal size, wash and pare. Boil in salted water until soft. Serve with drawn butter.

RICED YAM

Force hot boiled yam through a potato ricer, heap in a vegetable dish, salt and pepper, dot with pieces of butter.

YAM OMELETTE

Prepare mashed yam, turn in hot omelette pan greased with a tablespoon butter or olive oil, spread evenly. When browned underneath, fold as an omelette.

SCALLOPED YAM

Wash, pare and soak the yam. Slice in ¼-inch slices. Put in a greased baking dish, sprinkle with salt, pepper, and a little flour, dots of butter; repeat until dish is full. Cover with hot milk and bake until yam is soft.

YAMS HOLLANDAISE

3 cups diced yams	1 tablespoon lime juice
Fresh or canned chicken soup	Salt and pepper
⅓ cup butter	Parsley

Wash, pare, soak yams and cut in ½-inch dice. Cook diced yam in chicken soup stock until soft. (Canned chicken soup, strained, may be used.) Then drain. Cream together butter, lime juice, ½ teaspoon salt, ¼ teaspoon pepper. Add the yam, cook three minutes, cover with minced parsley or garnish with parsley leaves.

FRIED YAMS

Wash and pare yam, soak in cold water for an hour. Cut in dice. Take from water, dry between towels and fry in deep fat. Drain on brown paper and sprinkle with salt. Serve very hot.

YAM MARBLES

Wash and pare, cut with a French vegetable cutter into balls. Soak in cold salted water for half an hour. Dry between towels, drop in deep hot fat, drain and sprinkle with salt.

YAM CROQUETTES

2 cups hot riced yam	1 "culantro" leaf
2 tablespoons butter	1 clove garlic
½ teaspoon salt	1 teaspoon minced parsley pounded
¼ teaspoon pepper	together in a mortar
½ teaspoon celery seed	Yolk of one egg

Mix in order given, beating well. Shape, roll in corn meal, egg and meal again, fry one minute in deep hot fat, drain on paper.

YAM SAUTÉD

Slice cold boiled yam to make two cups. Cook a minced onion in 1½ tablespoons drippings or butter for a few minutes. Add 2 tablespoons more of the fat, put in the yam and cook until the yam has absorbed the fat, shaking so as to mix with the onion and take care it does not burn. Then add ½ tablespoon minced parsley.

YAM CURRY

3 cups cooked cubed yams	½ tablespoon curry
1 onion	½ tablespoon lime juice
¼ cup butter	Salt and pepper
½ cup meat or vegetable stock	

Cook onion finely chopped in butter until golden in color. Add cold boiled cubes of yam and cook until butter is absorbed. Then meat or vegetable stock, curry powder and lime juice, salt and pepper to taste. Let it cook until liquid is absorbed, but not too dry.

TANIER, YAUTIA, *Colocasia Esculenta*

TARO is the Polynesian name for our Puerto Rican *yautia* (*Colocasia esculenta*). In other places it is sometimes called *dasheen,* and it is the *eddo* of Barbadoes; *tannia, taya* and *oto* in other West Indian islands. *Dasheens, yautia, taros,* and *taniers* belong to the same botanical family as the calla-lily. The leaves of the taro resemble that lily; in the yautia the leaf is more arrow-shaped. The starchy tubers have long been a source of food in tropical countries and can be cooked and served in similar ways, boiled, baked, scalloped or fried.

In Puerto Rico there are four kinds of yautias, three of them species of *Xanthosoma,* a genus of aroids related to *Colocasia* but having the leaves hastate. They are known as "yautia blanca", "yautia amarilla" and "yautia palma" while the true taro is called "yautia malanga". When yautia is boiled it should remain in the water it is cooked in until sent to the table. Exposure to the air, if the water is poured off, makes it dry and tough. Many persons are not aware of the difference between similar root crops and it makes little difference from a cook's standpoint, excepting that it is good to know and recognize the varieties most rich in food values, for some are more nourishing than others.

YAUTIA

Follow any recipes as for potatoes. Yautias offer a cook many opportunities of using her ingenuity in experimenting.

YAUTIA SOUP

6 yautias	1 tablespoon flour
1 stalk celery	1 spray parsley
1 small onion	1 bay-leaf
1 tablespoon butter	Croutons
1 pint mint	

Peel yautias and boil with celery, onion, parsley, bay-leaf, and mint. When done rub through sieve, add milk, and flour and butter rubbed together. Serve hot with croutons.

YAUTIA AU GRATIN

Pare a yautia, cut in cubes, let boil ten minutes in salted water. Make two cups of white sauce; stir in yautia cubes, place in a baking dish, sprinkle lightly with buttered crumbs, and brown in oven.

On account of a large percent of protein, yautia has a higher food value than potato.

SAVORY YAUTIA

6 or 8 medium-sized yellow yautias	½ teaspoon salt
2 small onions	¼ teaspoon pepper
1 tablespoon chopped parsley	1 cup milk
1 heaping teaspoon butter	3 heaping tablespoons grated cheese

Put butter in saucepan with peeled and thinly sliced yautia in alternate layers with onion, parsley, salt and pepper. When all are in, add ½ cup water, let cook fifteen minutes with a cover on the saucepan. Then pour in the milk and let it cook another fifteen minutes. Lift onto a flat dish, scatter the cheese over it and let brown in the oven. This may also be cooked in a casserole in the oven.

MOLDED YAUTIA

Boil and mash yautia, season with salt, pepper and half a cup cream. Fill a baking powder can and chill. Slice in neat rounds, lay on a buttered pan and bake in the oven until brown.

YAUTIA PUFF

2 cups hot mashed yautia	½ cup milk
2 tablespoons butter	Salt and pepper
2 eggs	

Mix the yautia, well-beaten eggs, milk and seasoning to taste. Put in buttered baking dish and bake in hot oven until brown.

YAUTIA WITH MINT

Boil small yautias with a few leaves of mint. When done, drain and serve with drawn butter.

YAUTIA AND TURNIPS

Prepare as for mashed yautia, adding equal part of mashed turnips. Add three tablespoons butter to each pint of yautia and turnip, with salt and pepper to taste.

OLLA CALIENTE

Select six just ripe tomatoes, scald to loosen their skins; peel and cut into quarters or less. Put a layer in a casserole, then a layer of sliced onions, or very small onions no larger than a marble. Next a layer of sliced yautia, chopped parsley, then begin with another layer of tomatoes and continue with the different vegetables until the dish is full. Cover with meat stock, then let it boil or bake slowly for an hour. Serve peas and spinach, or else peas and asparagus with it.

YUCA—CASSAVA, *Manihot Utilissima*

"Li connait mange 'farine, pas connait plante' manioc."
(He knows how to eat the flour but not how to plant manioc.)
—An old Martinique proverb.

The cultivation of yuca dates far back; it forms a great bulk of the food of tropical countries. There are two varieties of the plant, one bitter and the other sweet. Bitter yuca contains a poisonous juice in which there is prussic acid which fortunately is dispelled by heat. The tubers are washed and peeled and then grated. The juice is pressed out and the meal is dried. Cassava bread is simply the fresh meal formed into thin cakes and dried on hot plates or pieces of tin held over a fire. The cassava is indigenous to these islands; it is mentioned in Columbus' journal as the Spaniards stocked their caravels with the bread on voyages returning to Spain. Ponce de Léon described the Borinquen Indians making bread, in one of his letters.

When the Indians cultivated their plantations, they, like most primitive peoples, had their own appropriate occupational songs. A Spanish translation from the Tainan, the prehistoric speech of the Puerto Rican Indians, goes as follows:

> "*Mi tierra tortolita,*
> *Ah, donde estará*
> *Pues yo no la veo*
> *Y mi corazón llora.*"

The origin of the Borinquen Indian is shrouded in mystery. He doubtless was a branch of the Arawaks, of the Antillean or Tainan culture, an immigrant to Puerto Rico. Archæologists believe other cultures preceded his. But the earliest records are those of the Spaniards, dating from the diary of Columbus. While the Caribs in neighboring islands were cannibals and warlike, the Borinquen fought only when attacked. He was essentially an agriculturist, tilling the fields and attentive to the natural products of the island. He even had a system of irrigation by canals.

The word "Borinquen" meant "Fatherland of powerful men." The stone implements made by the Borinquens represent the highest skill in perfection of stonework. Pestles and mortars, beads and pendants, balls, stools, and stone collars were peculiar to Puerto Rico. A remarkable thing is that the specimens found have been in such perfect condition, indicating faultless work. Kitchen middens have disclosed fine specimens of pottery, and some shell work as well. A very beautiful collection of stone articles was collected by the late George Latimer and is now in the Smithsonian Institution in Washington. Its perfection over other cultures is easily apparent.

The *Historia de las Indias* by Gomora, written in 1554, describes an Indian ceremony to bring crops. "Then there approached many women bearing baskets of cakes on their heads and many roses, flowers and fragrant herbs. They formed a circle as they prayed and began to chant something like an old ballad in praise of the God.

All rose to respond at the close of the ballad; they changed their tune and sang another song in praise of the cacique (the chief), after which they offered the bread to the idol, kneeling. The priests took the gift, blessed and divided it; and so the feast ended; but the recipients of the bread preserved it all the year and held that house unfortunate and liable to many dangers which was without it."

The agricultural people in all parts of the world have had their planting and harvest ceremonies. They believed in the corn-spirit or rice-spirit and made offerings to their gods to ensure good crops. In Puerto Rico the Borinquen Indians buried the Zemi, a three-pointed stone, with their cassava, as they believed the Zemi to be the messengers and mediators of the great God, and believed the crops would then be good. The same idea can be traced in most parts of the world, for folklore is rich in plant traditions.

A Spanish writer analyzed the significance of the word "yuca" as follows: "According to Las Casas the god of Haiti was called Yucahu Bagua Maorocati. Studying the syllables, yucayu is composed of Yuca and Yu. We know Yuca is the farinaceous tuber with which the Borinquen made bread called casabi. The syllable yu means white. Bagua means mar or sea. In maorocati we have a combination of roots; Ma means large, Ti, high, powerful; O is mountain. Roco is the verb which makes clear the attributes. That is to say, Maorocati means yuca blanca, great and powerful as the sea and the mountains. When we consider the difficulties, after growing and cultivating, grating and cooking, we cannot wonder that it was attributed to something god-like and mysterious, a plant which sustained and nourished but which also poisoned and killed if not treated properly. It was a terrible mystery for the simple imaginations of the people. The first explorers heard the Borinquen Indians speak of yuquiya, the yuca, and casabi, the white bread made from it, with veneration."

Oviedo in 1498 wrote of an alcoholic drink made from cassava.

The products from cassava are flour, starch, tapioca, glucose, alcohol, fertilizer and paper pulp.

Cassava bread is always to be found in market. Toast the bread to eat with tea or coffee. Grate it and put in glass jars as you would bread-crumbs, and use it in scalloped dishes, to thicken soups, and in any puddings where thickening is desired.

The root of the yuca is used as in any recipe for potatoes.

Tapioca is the farinaceous substance prepared from cassava. By undergoing heat of a certain temperature, the starch granules partially rupture and form into irregular pellets which become translucent when cold. In this condition the cassava starch forms the tapioca of commerce, a light, appetizing, digestible food used in puddings and soups.

YUCA BOILED

1½ pounds of yuca	4 teaspoons butter
4 cups water	Pepper to taste
1 teaspoon salt	1 teaspoon parsley minced

Wash the yuca with a vegetable brush. Peel and put in boiling salted water until soft, which will be 30 to 40 minutes. Serve hot with butter, salt and pepper. Garnish with the minced parsley.

YUCA MASHED

2 pounds yuca	4 teaspoons butter
2 teaspoons salt	½ cup milk

Boil the yuca, cut in small pieces, and mash smooth. Add the salt, butter and milk, beating well. It also may be put through a ricer.

YUCA CREAMED

Boil the yuca, cut in small pieces. Make a white sauce with 1 tablespoon flour, 1 tablespoon butter, 1 cup milk. Mix the yuca into the sauce and serve hot.

YUCA SOUP

2 pounds yuca	3 teaspoons salt
4 cups milk	¼ teaspoon pepper
4 teaspoons minced onions	¼ culantro leaf
2 teaspoons minced parsley	3 teaspoons butter
2 teaspoons flour	

Wash, boil and mash the yuca. Heat the milk and onion in a double boiler. Mix with the mashed yuca, cook ten minutes, then add the flour, salt and butter. Serve salt crackers as an accompaniment.

YUCA WITH TOMATO

1 teaspoon salt	6 strips bacon
½ pound yuca	3 large tomatoes

Boil the yuca and cut into pieces. Wrap each piece in a strip of bacon. Slice the tomatoes, put in a dripping pan and on each slice lay a piece of yuca wrapped in bacon. Then bake in the oven. May also be cooked in a frying-pan over the flame.

FRIED YUCA

1½ pounds yuca	2 teaspoons salt	Parsley

Boil the yuca and cut in three pieces. Fry lightly in a pan until golden brown. Serve hot with meat, adding parsley to garnish.

FRIED MASHED YUCA

1½ pounds yuca	½ cup milk
1 teaspoon salt	Chopped meat optional
1 tablespoon butter	

Boil yuca, mash smooth adding salt, butter, milk. Drop by tablespoonfuls into hot deep fat until brown. Chopped meat may be added to the yuca before frying and it may also have beaten egg and bread-crumbs added for variety.

YUCA CHIPS

Peel the yuca and slice thin as for potato chips. Lay in ice water half an hour. Dry with a towel and fry in deep hot fat. Drain on brown paper. Serve hot or cold.

FRENCH YUCA

Wash and peel the yuca, boil fifteen minutes. Cut in long pieces like French potatoes. Lay in iced-water half an hour. Dry in a towel, drop into deep, hot fat. Drain upon brown paper. Sprinkle with salt, serve hot with meat.

YUCA CROQUETTES

1½ pounds yuca	½ cup grated cheese
2 teaspoons salt	¼ cup minced olives
4 teaspoons butter	1 cup bread-crumbs
½ cup milk	2 eggs slight beaten
2 cups minced green peppers	

Boil and mash the yuca, add the butter, milk, salt, beaten egg. Beat well. Then add the peppers, cheese, olives and crumbs, form into croquettes and fry in deep fat.

YUCA BASKETS

4 cups mashed yuca	2 small bottles stuffed olives
1 cup flour	Watercress
4 eggs	2 teaspoons salt
3 cups white sauce	

Cook and mash the yuca, adding the flour, salt and eggs. Beat well and form into baskets. Fry in deep fat. Drain on brown paper. Make the white sauce. Fill the baskets, garnish with cress and olives. Serve hot as a luncheon dish.

YUCA SCALLOPED

1½ pounds yuca	2 cups chopped meat
1 cup bread-crumbs	1½ cups white sauce

Wash and cook the yuca, cut into sections and slices. Cover the bottom of a greased pan with bread-crumbs, then 1 cup yuca, ¾ cup white sauce, 1 cup meat, ¾ cup white sauce, ½ cup bread-crumbs. Bake in a hot oven an hour. Serve hot.

YUCA SOUFFLÉ

2 cups mashed yuca	1 cup milk or meat stock
4 eggs	1 teaspoon salt
3 teaspoons butter	Pepper to taste

Boil and mash the yuca. Melt the butter and add. Heat the milk, add salt, pepper and the mashed yuca. Beat the eggs and add. Turn into a greased mould and put in a moderate oven 25 or 30 minutes. Serve hot for luncheon.

YUCA SALAD

½ pound yuca	3 green peppers sliced
2 tomatoes	½ cup French dressing
1 head lettuce	2 beets
1 avocado	Olives

Boil the yuca, cut into dice. Arrange the lettuce in a flat bowl, put the peppers and beets (sliced) in center, and then around them put the yuca and avocado. Garnish with both green and ripe olives, pour over the French dressing.

DULCE DE YUCA

1 cup water	4 cups sugar
4 cups grated yuca	Vanilla

Wash, peel and grate the yuca, put in water and wash out the starch. Press until quite dry. Have equal parts of this meal and sugar, add the water, let it cook, stirring constantly. It is done when it leaves the sides of the saucepan. Add the vanilla, pour out onto a marble slab, cut in strips and serve for dessert.

CASSAVA MEAL

Two pounds yuca, washed, peeled, and grated. Add water to cover and stir it, working out all the starch. Put in an unbleached muslin bag, wring it hard to press out all moisture. Spread in a flat pan, dry it in a slow oven.

This meal is delicious to use as a thickening in soups, gravies and stews.

CASSAREEP

Cassareep is a dark brown liquid used in stews and meats for flavoring. It is made by boiling down the juice extracted by grating and squeezing out the moisture from the yuca. Some add "culantro" or other herbs and pepper. It is not unlike kitchen bouquet in flavor and like the papaya possesses the quality of rendering meat tender.

ANNATO

NUTS

CASHEW OR PAJUIL
(Anacardium Occidentale)

THERE are many varieties of the anacardium, the mango the best known, probably. But also belonging to this family are the sumac, poison-ivy, pistachio and cashew, widely distributed over the earth. One of the best known is the cashew or pajuil. One of the early voyagers said of this tree: "It furnishes food and household remedies to the poor, a refreshing beverage for the sick, resin and timber for industrial uses." Gabriel Soares de Souze, one of the early writers of Brazil, mentions a "fragrant and delicious wine" which the Indians made from the fruit. It is likely that it is indigenous to America and has been carried to other parts of the world.

This tropical tree is very ornamental and the wood is said to be very strong, useful in boat building. The leaves share with the poison-ivy the possession of an acrid juice very irritating to the mucous membrane. The nut is on the rosy fragrant fruit, growing outside at the blossom end. The irritating quality of the plant seems concentrated in this seed or nut, and it cannot be eaten raw on account of it. The poisonous quality is driven off by heat, so all nuts are roasted, when it becomes a delightful article of diet, rich and nutty in flavor. There can be made an indelible ink from the bark which can also be used in tanning. The gum from the bark can also be used as a tar for nets and boats. Two distinct oils can be extracted from the plant, one useful in medicine and the other keeps away insects. The oil was said to be a remedy for leprosy.

In the botanical gardens at Jamaica and Trinidad, the cultivation of this tree has been given much attention. The fruit is highly astringent and said to be of such value medicinally that in olden times dropsical slaves were permitted to go into a "cashew walk" or grove and eat the fruit and nuts, with great benefit. The fruit dried is a delicious confection, and was supposed to excite the faculties; especially memory, to such an extent that it was called "confection des sages". This may be eaten out of hand, it has a delicious aroma, and the juice being astringent is considered good for the stomach. The nuts after roasting may be salted.

OREJONES OR DRIED PAJUILES

Remove the nut from the fruit. Squeeze the juice from the fruit, cover fruit with water and boil. Pour off water, add cold water and let come to a boil again. Add as much sugar as there is fruit, boil down thick. Take each out on a board or tray, sprinkle with sugar and put in the sun to dry, covering with a sheet of glass. Put in the sun every day for a week.

ACHIOTE OR ANNATTO
(Bixa Orellana)

The seeds of this small tree yield a pasty coloring matter which gives a rich dye used to color butter and cheese. The export of annatto is a great industry in other islands. It was used by the Caribs to paint their faces and bodies. Formerly it was thought to have no food value but it lately has been discovered to contain a valuable vitamin. Used to color rice or vegetables in cooking it makes a dish attractive.

Fry a cupful of annatto seeds (achiote) in two cups of lard or crisco. Strain into a jar, and use this colored fat to flavor and color stews, gravy and soups.

ARACHIS HYPOGEA, PEANUTS OR MANÍ

Puerto Rican peanuts are small but very sweet; they can be used in a variety of ways and as substitute for other nuts. The little boys sell them on the street in one-cent packages. A favorite rhyme of these little "vendedores" goes as follows:

"Maní, maní, maní tostado,
No esá crudo ni está quemado,
Y yo lo vendo garantizado.
Un paquete de maní un centavo.
Maní, maní, llevo maní."

"Peanuts, peanuts, toasted peanuts,
They are neither raw nor burned,
And I sell them with a guarantee.
One package of peanuts for a cent.
Peanuts, peanuts, I carry peanuts."

ALMENDRA OR ALMOND

The native tree called almond is not a true almond which is related to the peach, but *Catappa terminalis*. While the nut is hard shelled and difficult to shell, it has a very good flavor and can be used in cooking.

HOW TO PEEL AND POUND ALMONDS

Put the almonds into boiling water; let them soak three minutes; strain, and lay them in cold water to cool thoroughly. Drain well again, and peel by pressing each almond between the thumb and fingers. Then put them into a sieve, and place them at the door of a slow oven to dry for ten minutes. Now pound them gently in a mortar, stirring well to prevent them from getting oily, and taking care to pound them very fine for at least ten minutes. Lay them on a cold dish and use when needed.

CREAM OF ALMOND SOUP

½ pound almonds	3 cups milk
3 tablespoons flour	Salt and red pepper
3 tablespoons butter	1 cup whipped cream

Skin almonds and pound in a mortar, or grind in a food-chopper with the nut butter attachment. Cream flour with butter, add milk and cook in a double boiler with the almonds twelve minutes. Add salt and a dash of red pepper. Pour into tureen over whipped cream and serve at once.

SUGARED ALMONDS
(An old Spanish Recipe)

Blanch the almonds and brown in the oven. Make a syrup with a cupful of sugar and a half cupful hot water. Let it boil until it threads, then put in the almonds and let it boil stirring thoroughly so that no syrup settles in the saucepan. When the sugar sets remove and separate the almonds one from another. Place in a tight bottle or glass jar to keep.

SALTED ALMONDS (OR PEANUTS)

Blanch the almonds and dry on a towel. Heat three-fourths cup olive oil, put in one-fourth of the almonds and fry until a delicate brown, stirring constantly. Remove and drain on brown paper and sprinkle with salt. Repeat until all are fried.

SESAME-PEANUTS-BRITTLE

1 cup brown sugar	½ cup puffed rice
1 cup honey or corn syrup	¼ cup sesame seeds
1 cup peanuts	Butter

Cook the syrup and sugar as for ordinary brittle, until it forms a ball when dropped in cold water. Then add rice, peanuts and sesame seeds. Pour in a buttered pan to cool.

AJONJOLÍ (SESAME) COOKIES

1 cup butter	½ teaspoon salt
2 cups sugar	2 teaspoons baking powder
2 eggs	2 tablespoons sesame seed
3 cups flour	

Cream the butter and sugar together, then add the beaten eggs and two cups water. Sift the flour, salt and baking powder, add the seeds. Roll thin on a floured board and put sesame seeds on top of each cookie, and bake on greased pans in a moderate oven.

COCONUT—*Coco Nucifera*

"I know not where his islands lift,
Their fronded palms in air,
I only know I cannot drift
Beyond his loving care."

—Whittier.

The coconut palm flourishes in all tropical countries. It is said that Father Diego Lorenzo brought the coconut palm to Puerto Rico from the Cape Verde Islands. Columbus speaks of palm trees he saw here, but it is probable they were the royal palms, for botanists seem to agree that the coconut was not indigenous to these islands.

Of all trees the coconut yields the greatest varieties of materials for the use of man. It provides shelter, food and even clothing. The nut yields oil, copra, coconut meal, coir, coconut milk for food. Coconut shells are used for utensils and a fine quality of charcoal. The leaves yield fiber, paper-stock, material for hats, baskets and thatch. From the trunk the wood is used for walking-sticks, construction and dugouts. There are many varieties, and while essentially a tree of the seashore, it grows in soil from sea-level to 3,000 feet above sea-level. The tree yields according to the soil; it is claimed that a tree may bear as many as 180 nuts in a year.

Grated coconut is high in food value. It is served as a vegetable or in salads and desserts. To make coconut cream, grate a coconut, pour a cup of boiling water over it, strain through a cheese-cloth squeezing out all the liquid. Let it stand overnight when the butter or cream will rise to the top. Skim, or drain off the water. The cream is delicious to use as a basis for salad dressing or instead of butter in pudding sauces.

"Coco de agua" is the water from the green coconut. Before the meat of the nut ripens, it is of a jelly-like consistency and the nut is full of a delicious fluid called "coco de agua". It possesses medical qualities. Those who drink it daily claim it keeps one in health, as well as being a refreshing drink. When picked from the tree which may be in the sun, it is surprising that the water is always cool and pleasant.

The green nut if left on the tree gradually ripens, when the water thickens, is absorbed in the nut meat and what is known as water in the green nut, turns into coconut milk.

A heavy ripe coconut has more liquid in it, usually, than the lighter in weight. By shaking, one may make sure it is full of liquid. Punch two of the eyes with an ice-pick to let in air and the liquid will then flow easily. Pour liquid into a dish and by inserting a butter-knife into the open eye, the nut will readily crack open if the knife is tapped with a hammer. Break into pieces and peel off the brown skin.

COCONUT

Grated coconut may be served as a vegetable with fish or meats. Add a little to stews for a change.

CAKE

1 cup flour	2 eggs
1 teaspoon baking powder	1 cup coconut milk
½ cup butter	1 cup grated coconut
¾ cup sugar	

Mix dry ingredients well, add the beaten eggs, coconut milk and coconut. Bake in a moderate oven. This is good for making cup cakes.

FILLING

½ cup coconut milk	4 tablespoons confectioner's sugar
1½ cups grated coconut	2 egg-whites

Mix ingredients with stiffly beaten egg-whites and spread. Do not cook.

FROSTING

1 teaspoon lime juice or lemon extract	2 cups sugar
1 cup grated coconut	1 teaspoon butter

Boil the sugar in half cup water until it reaches the soft ball stage; add butter, flavoring and half cup coconut. When cool, spread on cake and cover with remainder of the grated coconut.

CANDY

BALLS

Boil one cup sugar with milk of a coconut until a soft ball can be formed, then stir in as much grated coconut as will mix. Do not let it granulate. Drop from the point of a spoon on an oiled paper and make into flat cakes or round balls and roll in powdered chocolate.

CANDY

One pint granulated sugar, ¼ pint milk, ¼ pint grated coconut. Boil five minutes.

CREAM CANDY

Grate one coconut. To the milk of same add a pound and a half of sugar, heating slowly until dissolved. Then boil gently five minutes; add the grated coconut and boil ten or twelve minutes more. Stir all the while. Spread on buttered plates and set away until it hardens.

DROPS

One grated coconut, whites of 4 eggs beaten, ½ pound sifted sugar. Mix as thick as can just be dropped from a spoon.

MACAROONS

One freshly grated coconut, whites of two eggs, 2 cups powdered sugar. Stir the mixture over the fire until it thickens. Drop on oiled paper and brown in a hot oven.

PRALINE

Take a fresh coconut, break it open carefully and grate the meat. Put a cupful of white sugar, add enough water to melt, then add the coconut. Let it cook a moment, turning all the time. Beat and put in small cakes upon a china platter or marble slab to cool. Brown sugar may also be used in the same proportions.

TAFFY

Two cups sugar, ½ cup water boiled together; when it dissolves wash the sides of the pan and let it boil without stirring, until a soft ball can be formed on dropping it into cold water. Add 2 tablespoons of the "cream" made from the grated coconut, and a tablespoon full of lime juice. Let it boil until it hardens when dropped again into water, turn onto an oiled slab to cool, then mark into squares. This may also be pulled like molasses candy.

CUSTARD

Grated rind of 1 lemon or lime	½ cup sugar
1 coconut (see description)	4 eggs

Use a coconut that has the meat just "set". Slice the nut which should be jelly-like, stew it in its milk and add juice and grated rind of a lemon or lime, a half cup of sugar, beaten yolks of four eggs. Put into custard cups and bake. Make a meringue of the whites of the eggs beaten up light with sugar to sweeten, cover the custard and brown very slightly. Serve cold.

COCONUT IN CURRY

2 tablespoons olive oil	½ pint diced yautia
1 onion	½ pint diced carrots
1 tablespoon curry powder	½ pint peas
½ cup coconut milk	½ pint tomatoes
1 teaspoon salt	½ pint green pepper
Dry boiled rice	½ cup grated coconut

Coconut is much used in curries. To prepare a vegetable curry put two tablespoons olive oil in a saucepan, slice an onion into it and let cook. Add a tablespoon of curry powder mixed with half a cup of coconut milk, a teaspoon salt and mix with the onion.

Have prepared beforehand half of a pint each, diced yautia, carrots, peas, tomatoes, green pepper, then add half cup of grated coconut. Let simmer together and serve with dry boiled rice.

DULCE

1 coconut	1 lime
1½ cups sugar	

Grate the coconut, add two cups water, sugar, skin and juice of one lime and let cook slowly until it thickens a bit.

FRITTERS

3 tablespoons flour	4 eggs
Coconut milk	1 cup grated coconut

Scald flour with coconut milk to make a stiff paste. When cool add four egg-yolks and the whites of two, a cup of grated coconut. Mix well and drop by spoons into hot deep fat.

PRESERVES

Scrape the tender meat from a coconut not yet ripe, cut in small shreds. Drop into a syrup made by boiling 1½ cupfuls sugar with ¾ cupful water and cook ten minutes or so. Serve cold. A few drops lime juice or lemon juice may be added.

"BIEN ME SABE" (It tastes good to me)
(MISS JOSEFINA NOBLE)

1 coconut	Sponge cake or lady fingers
1½ cups sugar	Sherry wine
3 eggs	

Break a coconut saving all the milk. Grate the nut and squeeze out all the juice and add the milk. Make a syrup with a cup and a half of sugar and a cup of water. Let it cool and add it to the coconut milk. Add the beaten yolks of three eggs and cook in a double-boiler stirring constantly until it gets to a creamy consistency. Line a glass bowl with sponge cake or lady fingers dipped in sherry wine and pour over it the coconut cream.

COCONUT CORNSTARCH PUDDING

2 tablespoons powdered sugar	1 cup sugar
Lemon or lime juice	Cornstarch
1 coconut	

Extract cream from a grated coconut, put it over the fire with a cup of sugar and enough cornstarch to make a soft cream, cooking it in a double-boiler. When done let it cool. For the sauce take the milk saved in breaking the coconut, flavor with a tablespoon of powdered sugar and a little lemon or lime juice. Pass this with the pudding and add to each serving a tablespoon of grated coconut that has been toasted in the oven, mixed with a tablespoon of powdered sugar.

COCONUT-TOMATO SOUP

Make tomato soup by the ordinary method, using milk of the coconut, or cream made by extracting the cream from the grated nut, instead of fresh milk. Or use canned tomato soup, adding the same quality of coconut milk. This has a delightful flavor.

COCONUT ICE

1 ripe coconut	1 lime
1 cup sugar	

Grate a fresh ripe coconut, pour over it one pint of boiling water. Squeeze through a cheese cloth, extracting all of the juice. Add the milk saved in opening the nut, one cup of sugar, juice and grated rind of lime and freeze in an ice cream freezer.

COCONUT ICE CREAM

Follow the same procedure as for coconut ice, adding a cup of cream.

BANANA AND PLANTAIN

THE origin of the banana is unknown; it is probably as old as human records, evolved in the infancy of the race and found throughout the tropics. Recent finds in gypsum deposits of the Tertiary Age in southern France disclose the banana to be a most primitive plant and similar to those found in Abyssinia. In Puerto Rico the tradition exists that they were introduced from the Dark Continent. Some bear names such as "Congo" and "Guineo" and it may be that they were carried by ocean currents or in some earlier intercourse between the Old and the New Worlds. No lovelier plant can be imagined than the banana, the sturdy stalks bearing a crown of enormous light green leaves, always moving in the tropic breeze. Somerset Maugham called them the "tattered habiliments of an empress in adversity." Truly royal they are in coloring and dignity, and even when tattered and torn by every wind that blows they are one of the glories of the Tropics. Puerto Rico does not ship many bananas but an immense quantity is consumed locally, being called "the poor man's bread." Nothing is more conveniently and easily prepared, considering the fact that the poor have no ovens, the cooking being done on charcoal braziers.

The fruit of the plantain, peeled and toasted, is delicious and nourishing when eaten like bread. Roasted or fried they are always combined with other foods. They are generally cooked while still green, but if allowed to mature they become yellow and black. Flour is made by drying and grinding the plantain; used in gruels, it is most acceptable in stomach disorders and it is so easily digested that it may be given to babies.

It is said that there are more than forty varieties of plantains and bananas grown on the island. The plantain is used as a vegetable, for it requires cooking, and the banana either as a fruit or vegetable, being more succulent and of finer flavor and creamy texture. Both plantain and banana are species of the genus Musa. Not only are they valuable for the food value, but they are one of the most prolific plants known. Buckle calculated that an acre planted will support more than fifty persons, whereas the same amount of land planted with wheat in Europe, will only support two persons. Its produce is forty-four times greater than that of potatoes and one hundred and thirty-three times greater than that of wheat.

The banana is propagated by planting the suckers and the total time from planting to fruiting ranges from nine to fourteen months. Each trunk bears one bunch of bananas. Unlike many fruits the banana is ripened cut off from the plant. The people who live in the Tropics cut off a bunch and hang it in a cool part of the house, removing the bananas as fast as they ripen.

GUINEOS DÁTILES WITH CHEESE

Fry dátiles in butter until brown. Split with knife and insert a slice of fried cheese.

BANANA PIE

Ripe bananas	3 eggs
Pie crust	3 heaping tablespoons of sugar
1 pint milk	for custard
2 heaping tablespoons cornstarch	3 tablespoons sugar for meringue

Line your pie plate with a good crust and bake it a light brown. Cover the bottom of the crust with a thick layer of sliced ripe bananas. Pour over these a custard made as follows: To one pint of boiling milk add two heaping tablespoons of cornstarch dissolved in cold milk; the yolks of three eggs and three heaping tablespoonfuls of sugar. Flavor with vanilla. Pour over this a meringue made of the whites of three eggs and three tablespoonfuls of sugar beaten very stiff. Brown the meringue. Serve cold.

SLICED BANANAS

Bananas may be served sliced or whole by pouring sweetened cream over them.

BANANA SNOW

2 good-sized tablespoons	1 pint boiling water
Knox Gelatine	1 orange (pulp)
1½ cups sugar	Juice of 2 lemons
½ cup cold water	

Dissolve the gelatine in the cold water and when it is dissolved add sugar, boiling water and lemon juice, strain and set away to get thick, then beat up the whites of three eggs, and pour the gelatine in and beat all to a foam. Put in mould with layers of bananas and orange and set away to get cold. To be eaten with custard.

BANANA WHIP

1½ envelope Knox Sparkling Gelatine	½ cupful sugar or syrup
¼ cupful cold water	½ cupful chopped nuts or
4 tablespoonfuls of lemon juice	½ cupful of crumbs (toasted
1 cupful of boiling water	or cookie crumbs)
1 cupful of banana pulp (about 2 bananas)	

Soak the gelatine in cold water for five minutes. Put the sugar or syrup in the boiling water, boil for one minute and add to the softened gelatine. Cool. Add the lemon juice to the banana pulp and mash until blended. Beat the gelatine mixture until it is frothy and about the thickness of whipped cream. Add the banana pulp. Whip until blended. Add the nuts or crumbs, and pour into wet mould or individual dishes. Chill. Serve with milk or cream, or on lettuce with salad dressing.

BANANA SALAD

Split bananas lengthwise, serve on a crisp lettuce. They may be sprinkled with finely chopped nuts or sesame seeds; they may be combined with dates, prunes or other dried fruits or combined with almost any other fruit. Serve with a boiled dressing to which whipped cream has been added or a plain French dressing.

BANANA OMELETTE

Beat yolks of three eggs with a half cup of sugar, a pinch of salt and the mashed pulp of three bananas. Fold in the beaten whites of the three eggs and cook in an omelette pan.

BANANA FRITTERS

Slice bananas and squeeze lemon juice over them, then dip in fritter batter, and fry in deep fat.

BANANA AND GROSELLAS

To a cupful of stewed and strained *grosellas* (gooseberries) add a cupful of mashed banana. Add a cupful of sugar and cook slowly until done.

FROZEN BANANAS

6 bananas   1 orange
2 limes   2 egg-whites

To six mashed bananas add the juice of two limes, the juice of one orange, sweeten to taste and freeze. When partially frozen add the beaten whites of two eggs and finish freezing.

LA COMPOSITE

Bananas peeled and sliced thin, sprinkled with sugar, with alternate layers of orange, peeled and sliced thin with sugar; set on ice before using.

BROILED BANANAS
To Serve with Steaks

Peel one large banana and one-half, and divide into six strips. Broil over a clear fire until hot through. Arrange a spoonful of horseradish sauce on each round of steak; over this place a section of broiled banana and garnish the dish with cress.

FRIED BANANAS

Cut bananas into any shape, roll in a beaten egg, then in bread-crumbs, and cook until brown in hot, deep lard or cottolene.

PLANTAIN

Plantains are those varieties of banana that cannot be eaten raw, but require cooking and are used as a vegetable.

FRIED GREEN PLANTAIN

Fry in a little butter until brown and sprinkle with sugar, a little cinnamon and nutmeg.

FRIED YELLOW PLANTAIN

Soak two plantains in salt water for two hours, fry in butter until tender. Sprinkle half a cup of sugar over them while hot.

PLATANUTRI

Select very green plantains, cut them across in very thin slices as you would potato chips. Plunge in iced salt water a short while, then dry and fry in deep fat. Serve as an accompaniment to drinks.

BAKED PLANTAIN

Ripe plantains are baked in the oven and served whole with meat. They may also be sliced thin and wrapped around small pieces of beef filet, then baked.

TOSTONES

Take green plantains, cut them diagonally in inch slices. Lay in salt water five minutes. Put on to fry, when soft remove to a piece of brown paper, put another piece of brown paper over and with a blow of the fist squash the slices flat. Return to the pan to resume frying until a golden brown in color. Serve hot as a vegetable.

PIOUS NUNS

3 ripe plantains	1 tablespoon capers
½ cup minced meat	6 olives
¼ cup minced onions	2 tablespoons lard
¼ cup minced tomato	1 teaspoon salt
1 egg	Achiote
1 cup bread-crumbs	

Wash the plantain, cut in four long slices, fry in lard until brown. Form a circle with each slice, holding in place with wooden toothpicks. Cook the meat in shortening five minutes. Add the other ingredients, let cook together five minutes. Fill the plantain circles with the meat mixture. Cover with the bread-crumbs, beaten egg and again with crumbs, or else with the following paste:

¾ cup flour	1 teaspoon baking powder
¼ teaspoon salt	⅓ cup milk
1 egg	

Then fry in a pan until brown, serve hot as a luncheon dish.

BAKED PIE

3 plantains	1½ teaspoon salt
1 cup milk	½ pound meat
⅓ cup butter	¼ cup minced onion
¼ cup green pepper minced	2 tablespoons raisins
2 eggs hard-boiled	12 olives
Pepper to taste	

Boil and mash the plantains. Fry the chopped meat lightly. Add the onion, pepper, slices hard-boiled eggs, olives, raisins; cook five minutes more. Grease a Pyrex mould, put in half the mashed plantains. Then put in the meat mixture and cover with the other half of the plantain; brown in the oven for twenty minutes. A good luncheon dish.

DULCE DE AMARILLO

4 cups milk   1 yellow plantain
3 cups sugar   2 pieces cinnamon
                ½ teaspoon lemon skin

Wash, peel and cut the plantain in slices ½-inch thick. Add the milk and
sugar to the plantain. Put to cook on a moderate flame until soft, and the
milk forms grains. Serve cold as a dessert.

BOILED PLANTAIN

3 plantains   ⅓ cup butter
2 teaspoons salt   4 tablespoons olive oil

Wash and cook in a steamer. Serve hot with the butter or oil, salt and
pepper.

MASHED PLANTAIN

3 plantains   ¼ cup butter
2 teaspoons salt   ¼ cup milk
                Pepper

Cook and mash the plantains adding the butter, milk salt and pepper. Mash
them well and serve hot. This may also be put through a vegetable riser.

PLANTAIN BALLS

1 green plantain   1 tablespoon flour
½ teaspoon salt   3 tablespoons minced beef
2 teaspoons lard   1 tablespoon minced onion
½ garlic clove   6 olives
1 teaspoon minced pepper   Capers' anchiote
                2 teaspoons minced tomato

Peel the plantain, lay in salt water for five minutes, then grate. Add salt,
melted lard, achiote and flour. Fry together the meat, tomato, garlic, pepper,
olives, capers. Make six balls of the grated plantain, make a hole in each and
fill it with the meat mixture. Drop into hot soup to cook thirty minutes and
serve with the soup. They may also be served as an entrée.

PLANTAIN OMELETTE

2 ripe plantains   6 tablespoons milk
6 eggs   Chopped parsley
½ teaspoon salt   Pepper

Wash and peel the plantains, cut in slices ¼-inch thick. Fry in a little
shortening. Separate the eggs and to the yolks add the salt, pepper and milk,
beating all together. Beat the whites until light and add to the yolks. Add
the plantain and pour into a greased omelette pan. When set, turn over one-
half onto the other and let cook until brown. Serve hot for luncheon.

AREPITAS
(Kind of a Griddle Cake)

1 cup mashed ripe plantain	1 tablespoon Crisco
2 eggs	1 tablespoon sugar
1 cup milk	1 teaspoon baking powder
¼ teaspoon salt	¼ teaspoon powdered cinnamon
1 cup flour	

Boil the plantain. Separate the eggs. To the yolks add the salt, baking powder and Crisco, beat well. Add the milk, beat again. Then add the plantain, the flour and cinnamon, last of all the beaten whites of the eggs. Fry on a griddle turning once. Serve hot with honey, syrup or guava jelly.

CROQUETTES

3 plantains, green or ripe	½ teaspoon cinnamon
1 tablespoon butter	3 eggs
½ teaspoon sugar	1 teaspoon salt
½ cup bread-crumbs	

Wash the plantains, cook until soft; peel and mash while hot. Add half the eggs beaten, butter, salt, cinnamon and sugar. Mold into croquettes, roll in bread-crumbs, then in egg, again in bread-crumbs. Fry in hot fat. Drain on brown paper and serve hot for luncheon with guava jelly.

BAKED WITH CINNAMON

3 ripe plantains	½ teaspoon cinnamon
¼ cup water	⅛ cup butter
1 cup grape juice or wine	¾ cup sugar
1 teaspoon lemon juice	

Wash the plantains, boil until soft. Grease a mould with butter, put in the plantains, add the lemon juice, wine, cinnamon and water. Let bake until done. Serve either hot or cold.

MAYAGUEZ ROSE

3 cups mashed plantain	12 stuffed olives
¼ cup minced green peppers	1 hard-boiled egg
½ cup minced sweet red peppers	Salt and pepper

Cook and mash the plantains, spread it on a large plate. Separate the yolk from the white of the egg and cut into pieces. Decorate the plantain with the yolk, the whites around the yolk, then the green pepper and around that the red pepper, so that the plate resembles a rose. Sprinkle with salt and pepper. Around the edge put the olives. Serve cold as a luncheon dish.

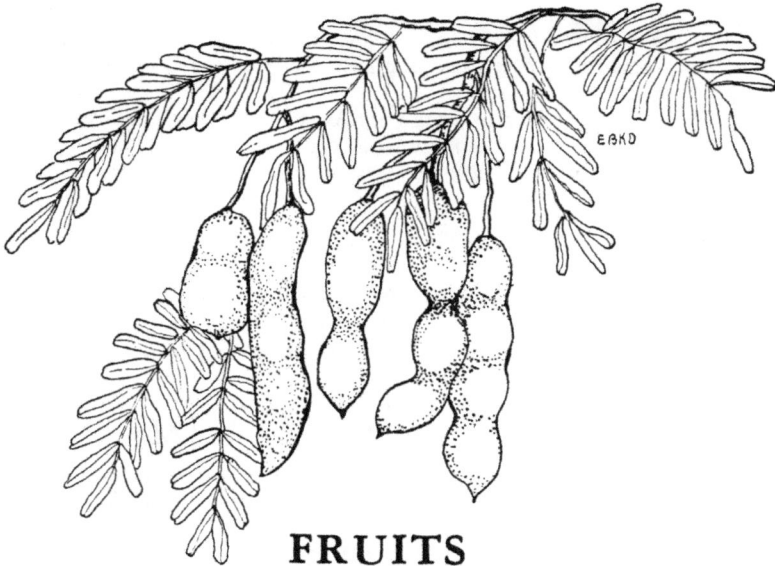

FRUITS

*"If then the tree may be known by the fruit,
As the fruit by the tree."—Henry IV.*

Two of the most wholesome and important articles of food are fruits and vegetables; and where it is possible to have them every day in the year, the products of the country should be served daily. Fruits supply a variety of acids which invigorate the system and keep the blood in condition.

Fruits should be carefully washed before eating, or before putting them away in an ice-box. Almost any of the native fruit juices can be canned or preserved for use during the months they may be out of season. Pineapple, for example, is an easily made dessert at much less expense than the commercial canned fruit.

Fruit soups are served cold, chilled on ice if possible, in small glasses or glass bowls or bouillon cups.

Stewed fruit may be strained through a sieve, thickened a bit with cornstarch, arrowroot or cassava. Cook till clear, add sugar and a little lemon juice.

ANONA SQUAMOSA

Anon was the name given by Borinquen Indians to this fruit. Its early home was without doubt the West Indies. In 1692 one of the early friars wrote of it: "The pulp is very white, tender, delicate, and so delicious that it unites to agreeable sweetness a most delightful fragrance like rose-water, and if presented to one unacquainted with it he would certainly take it for a blanc-mange." Unlike the soursop, it is never made into preserves, nor is it used for sherbets, but served simply as a fruit.

The sugar apple is also found in Asiatic countries, and representations of the fruit have been found in carvings and wall paintings in ancient ruins of India. There are several varieties of this fruit. It is distinctly a dessert fruit.

CORAZON—CUSTARD APPLE
Anona reticulata

This fruit is more oval and smaller than the guanábana. The flesh is yellow. It is very palatable if iced, served with a bit of lime juice squeezed over it.

CUSTARD APPLE ICE CREAM

Remove the seeds and skin from three custard apples. Scald one pint of milk and add one cupful sugar. When cold, put the fruit in and freeze.

GUANÁBANA OR SOURSOP
Anona muricata

There are many varieties of the Anona family, the most popular being the Soursop or "Guanábana", which has a rough green skin, enclosing a soft juicy white pulp, in which are imbedded shiny black seeds. The fruit is the largest of the anonas and unrivalled for drinks and sherbets. An infusion of the leaves of the plant is said to be a remedy for dysentery. The fruit itself is cooling and refreshing.

GUANÁBANA ICE

Crush the white pulp of the fruit, add a bit of lime juice, strain, and freeze, using at least one cup of sugar and a large lime to each pint of fruit.

GUANÁBANA REFRESCO

Open the guanábana, take out the core and peel, putting the pulp in a colander and pressing out the seeds. For a pound of fruit pulp, add a pound of sugar, juice of a lime and water to taste.

CHAMPOLA DE GUANÁBANA

Prepare as for "refresco", and use milk instead of water. This makes it richer to the taste and more nutritious as well.

GUANÁBANA SHERBET

Peel and mash a guanábana, removing seeds. To a pint of fruit, add the same quantity of sugar, juice of a lime, and a pint or more of water. Mix and freeze.

THE AGUACATE—AVOCADO

Persea gratissima

The avocado belongs to the laurel family and is, therefore, related to the cinnamon, camphor and sassafras. It is indigenous to the mainland of tropical America, and was first mentioned in European annals by González Hernández de Oviedo in 1526, who saw the tree in Colombia near the Isthmus of Panama. Pedro de Ciega de León reports it in 1532 as used by the Spanish explorers. In composition it is more of a nut than fruit since it contains 1.5 to 2.5 percent protein, and 13 to 22 percent oil. There is practically no sugar or starch in it. The name *Aguacate* is an adaption of the Aztec name of the fruit.

Hernández, a physician, sent by the King of Spain to study the medical plants of Mexico, speaks of it in 1615. The trees grow to a great size, the fruit is larger than the average pear, resembling the northern fruit in name and shape only. Its color is a bright grass-green, although some varieties have a reddish brown cheek, and the seed is also very curious, being about two inches in diameter.

An avocado must be quite ripe when ready for use, and then gives to slight pressure of the thumb, and should be used at once. It has a delicious nutty taste, making a nutritious substitute for animal fat. As with olives, once liked they prove a choice delicacy. Though there are many ways of preparing avocados as a salad, using the hollow of a half to hold the salad mixtures, the more simple forms of serving are the preferred ways in the South.

Avocado is sometimes served as a dessert with wine dressing, and it is used cubed or in thin slices in soup, but it seems essentially a fruit salad.

AVOCADO SALADS

Take two mustard spoonfuls of French mustard, half a teaspoonful salt, dash of pepper, a tablespoonful of vinegar and two of oil. Put a spoonful in each avocado's half, and a piece of ice to serve.

Another method of serving is to mash, add plenty of French dressing, fill the shells with mixture and chill thoroughly before sending to the table.

It is good served in combination with other salads such as cucumbers, cress, lettuce, onions or beets, on crisp lettuce.

As a delicate sandwich accompaniment to salads, mash an avocado, add vinegar or lemon juice, salt, pepper and Worcestershire sauce, spread on thin slices of bread.

THREE FRUITS SALAD

2 avocados	½ cup diced banana
Lettuce	French dressing
¾ cup diced pineapple	

Cut avocados in half and scoop out the pulp. Line shell with crisp lettuce leaves and fill with the avocados, pineapple and banana, cut in dice and mixed with French dressing.

SALAD CUP

½ cup seedless raisins	French dressing
2 medium-sized grapefruit	Lettuce
2 avocados	Mayonnaise

Wash the raisins and slice. Peel the grapefruit and divide into sections, removing all the white membrane; cut into small pieces. Peel the avocados and cut each half in two circles with a cooky cutter. Hollow out the centers of circles. Combine the trimmings with the raisins and grapefruit and marinate in French dressing. Place the avocados circles on the lettuce, fill with marinated mixture, and top with the mayonnaise. Makes eight salads.

AVOCADO SALAD No. 1

After chilling the pears on ice, cut in halves, remove the large seed, serving one-half to a person. A simple dressing of oil, lemon juice, sugar, salt and pepper, is all that is necessary. Crisp lettuce leaves or cress make a dainty garnish.

AVOCADO SALAD No. 2

A more elaborate Spanish salad is made by cutting the pears in rings, instead of halving, and scattering over them thin slices of ripe tomato, and crisp cucumber. Dress with salt, pepper, oil and lemon juice.

AVOCADO SALAD No. 3

Cut two avocados into cubes. Chop one green pepper very fine. Throw French dressing over all.

AVOCADO SALAD No. 4

Peel and cut two avocados into cubes. Chop very fine together, one onion, one pepper and one tomato. Mix with the cubes of avocados and serve on lettuce with French dressing.

CITRUS FRUITS—*Rutaceae*

There is perhaps no fruit of more value than the citrus fruits; their beauty, refreshing effects and general health-giving qualities make them deservedly popular.

LEMONS

Lemons were known to the ancient Greeks and Romans and introduced by the Arabs into Spain. By the Shipping Act of 1867 every British ship going to countries where lemon or lime juice could not be obtained, was required to take sufficient to give one ounce to every member of the crew daily. It is from this custom that the Britishers got the name of "limey".

A lemon contains from four to five tablespoonfuls of juice. If you wish to use only a little juice, don't cut the lemon in halves, make a small incision and squeeze out the amount you need. The rest of the lemon will then keep better and will not dry up.

Dried lemon peel is good in fruit cake; cut it in small pieces with scissors.

Lemon juice is much better than vinegar in making salad dressing.

Try lemon juice and sugar on lettuce, sometimes, as a change from salad dressings.

The juice of a lemon in a small cup of black coffee without sugar will often cure a headache, if taken first thing in the morning.

LEMON SYRUP

To a pint of lemon juice add a pint of water and two and one-half pounds of sugar. Add a little of the grated rind and let it simmer on a slow fire. Bottle and keep in the ice-box to be used for drinks as needed.

CANDIED LEMON PEEL

Follow recipe for crystallized grapefruit peel.

LEMON PUDDING

1 tablespoon butter	1 cup milk
4 tablespoons sugar	2 egg-whites
1 lemon	

Mix one tablespoon of butter with four tablespoons of sugar. Add grated rind of one lemon and juice of one-half lemon. Add one cup of milk and fold in the stiffly beaten whites of two eggs. Pour into a buttered baking dish and bake thirty minutes in a moderate oven. This pudding may be served hot or cold. This recipe is always a surprise the first time it is tried because a delicate spongy crust forms with a rich lemon sauce below.

LEMON PIE FILLING

3 eggs   1 lemon
¾ cup sugar   Cooked pastry shells

Cook slowly in a double-boiler until thick, three egg-yolks, one-half a cup of sugar, and the juice and grated rind of one lemon; when done, this mixture will look like scrambled eggs. Set it aside to cool. Beat the egg-whites stiff; add a pinch of salt and one-fourth cup of sugar; fold the cooked egg mixture into this. Pour this mixture into cooked pastry shells and leave in the oven until the top is brown. This same mixture can be used as a cake filling, or as a dessert by itself, by chilling in sherbet glasses.

FLAX-SEED LEMONADE

Into a quart of boiling water put a cupful of flax-seed. Add a little sugar and the juice of two lemons. Let it stand in a covered jar two hours and drink it hot on retiring. Fine for colds.

LEMON CORDIAL

(An Old French Recipe)

Pare the yellow skin from two dozen lemons, let it stand twenty-four hours in a gallon of French brandy. Then take the lemons, roll them and squeeze the pulp and juice. Strain, and when the lemon skins are ready, mix the brandy with the lemon juice, adding three pints of milk scalding hot. Let stand twenty-four hours and then put into bottles.

ORANGES

"Thus go the cries of Rome's fair town,
First they go up street, then they go down;
Buy oranges,—No better sold,
New brought in Spanish ships;
As yellow bright as minted gold,
As sweet as ladies' lips."

The orange is said to have originated in India and from there spread to western Asia and eventually Europe. In the twelfth century the Crusaders carried it into Italy. An orange tree is shown at the monastery of St. Sabina at Rome having been planted there by St. Dominic. On Columbus' second voyage he brought orange seeds to the West Indies, for planting. The orange seems to have imprisoned the gold of each day's sunlight with all its fragrance and glow. It is said the first oranges were imported into England by Sir Walter Raleigh.

TAPIOCA ORANGE PUDDING

6 oranges ½ cup tapioca Thin custard

Cut the oranges so as to make baskets, scooping out the inside pulp without breaking the shells. Squeeze the juice from the pulp and strain. Soak half a cup of tapioca in this for one hour, cook slowly until a clear jelly. Fill the skin baskets half full of this jelly when it is cold. Put on the ice and serve very cold with a thin custard.

ORANGE FLOAT

2 le.nons 5 oranges
1½ cups sugar Meringue
4 tablespoons cornstarch

Heat one quart of water, the juice of two lemons and one and one-half cupfuls of sugar. When boiling, stir into it four tablespoonfuls of cornstarch rubbed smooth in a very little water. Cook until the whole is thickened and clear. When cool, stir into the mixture five nice oranges which have been sliced and freed from seeds and all the white portions. Meringue and serve cold.

COMPOTE OF ORANGES

1 handful loaf sugar 6 oranges 1 glass brandy

Put a handful of loaf sugar to boil with a gill (½ cup) of water in a saucepan; when it boils add the rind of three oranges chopped fine. Let boil five minutes, add a glass of brandy and pour the syrup hot over half a dozen oranges that have been peeled and sliced with the seeds picked out. Leave the oranges in a dish with the syrup until quite cold.

ORANGE FRAPPPÉ

1 pint orange juice 1 pint sugar Juice 2 lemons

Make a syrup by boiling one quart water and one pint sugar 26 minutes. Add orange and lemon juices; cool; strain and freeze. For freezing use equal parts of rock salt and finely crushed ice.

ORANGE SALAD

Remove sections of orange neatly, arrange on a lettuce or water cress, sprinkle with small leaves of mint, cover with French dressing made with lime juice instead of vinegar.

ORANGE MILK SHERBET

1 cup sugar 1 cup orange juice
½ cup water 1 tablespoon lemon or lime juice
¼ teaspoon salt 1 cup evaporated milk

Boil sugar, water and salt, add fruit juices and freeze. When half frozen, add evaporated milk and continue freezing.

ORANGES PRESERVED WHOLE
(ELSIE DOMENECH)

Grate slightly the rinds of firm sweet oranges, sufficiently to take off some of the oil, but leave them yellow. Stew until tender, cool them and drop into boiling syrup, in the proportion of a pound of sugar to a pound of fruit. When nicely done, they are whole, transparent, and ornamental.

ORANGE JELLY

Select tart oranges, press out the juice, and mix it with an equal quantity of juice pressed from sub-acid apples. Then for each pint of juice use from three-quarters to one pound of sugar, and process the same as in directions for making other jellies.

ORANGE OMELETTE

3 eggs	1 tablespoon butter
1 tablespoon powdered sugar	1 orange

Separate the whites and yolks of the eggs. To the well-beaten yolks add one tablespoonful powdered sugar, grated rind of an orange and three tablespoonfuls of the juice. Beat the whites very stiff and fold into this. Melt one tablespoonful butter and when hot, turn into the mixture. Brown very carefully in an omelette pan. Cover the omelette with powdered sugar.

ORANGE SOUFFLÉ

1 quart milk	2 large oranges
6 eggs	Sugar
Vanilla	

Make a custard of one quart of milk and the yolks of six eggs, sweetened to taste. Pour this, boiling hot, over the grated rind, pulp and juice of two large oranges, which have been previously sweetened a little to prevent curdling the custard. Put this in the oven, and bake until stiff enough to hold the meringue. Beat the whites with one-third of a cupful of sugar, and flavor with vanilla. Put on the meringue as roughly as possible, and set it again in the oven to brown slightly. If the oranges are very juicy, use one less.

ORANGE CHIFFON PIE

4 eggs	1 cup sugar
Grated rind and juice of 1 lemon	Grated rind and juice of ½ small orange
1 medium-sized baked pastry shell	

Beat the whites of the eggs until firm. Fold into them one-half cup of the sugar and let stand while preparing a custard with the yolks of the eggs, remaining sugar, and grated rind and juice of lemon and orange. Place in double boiler and cook until it thickens, stirring constantly. Fold carefully into the beaten whites and sugar just enough to blend. Pour into a baked pastry shell.

ORANGE PUNCH

To a glass of orange juice, add a well-beaten egg and sugar to taste. Pour over cracked ice in a tall glass.

ORANGE ICE

To a pint of orange juice add a pint of water and two cups of sugar. Freeze.

ORANGE PUFFS

⅓ cup butter	1¾ cups flour
1 cup sugar	2 eggs
½ cup milk	2 level teaspoons baking powder

Mix above ingredients as for Cottage Pudding and bake in small tins. Serve with hot orange sauce.

HOT ORANGE SAUCE

Juice 1 lemon	½ cup sugar
1 cup orange juice	1 tablespoon cornstarch

Mix cornstarch slowly in juices and cook until slightly thickened.

ORANGE MARMALADE

Peel half of the quantity of oranges you intend using and discard this peel. Cut the pulp in fine pieces, removing seeds and core. Quarter and slice remaining half of oranges, without peeling. Mix and weigh. Put a pint of cold water to a pound of fruit; let stand 24 hours. Heat and simmer till soft, set aside. Weigh and take equal amount of sugar, heat separately. Add hot sugar to fruit and simmer until the fruit cooks clear and syrup thickens when tested in ice water. Bottle and seal hot.

ORANGE MERINGUE CUSTARD

1 cup condensed milk	2 oranges	2 eggs

This dessert is made by blending one cup of sweetened condensed milk with diced pulp and juice of two oranges. Add two well-beaten egg-yolks. Pour into buttered baking dish. Cover top with meringue made from the stiffly beaten egg-whites sweetened with two tablespoons of sugar. Bake fifteen minutes, or until meringue is brown, in moderately slow oven (325 degrees F).

ORANGE—WHOLE

Serve oranges whole for breakfast. With a sharp knife cut off the peel, taking off all the white inner skin. Plunge a fork into the end where the sections come together and, turning the fork as you eat, you get every bit of the fruit.

SEVILLE ORANGE OR NARANJA

"Fine Sevil oranges, fine lemons, fine,
Round, sound and tender, inside and rined,
One pin's prick their vertue show:
They're liquor by their weight, you know."

—London Cry of Nell Gwynne, the favorite mistress of King Charles the Second, who grew up in the humble occupation of "orange woman", made famous by Ben Jonson.

The *naranja* or wild sour orange is the Seville orange, brought into the Island by Columbus for planting in the New World and carried all through Spanish America by the early explorers. The origin of this fruit is uncertain; some attribute it to China, others to the Himalayas; the Moors, doubtless, took it to Spain, planting it in quantities around in the city of Seville, from whence it acquired its name.

It has formed an important article of commerce as great amounts of oil are extracted from its leaves, and from its flowers—oil of Neroli, used in perfumes and liquors. Curaçao is made from this fruit. It deserves wider cultivation and use in the household. It makes excellent lemonade, and can be used in any recipe calling for lemons. The leaves steeped make a tea that is a fine tonic. If very ripe the fruit, cut in two like grapefruit, can be served in its place and it is superior to all fruits if served thinly sliced for tea.

In fact, it can be used in any way the other citrus fruits are used; it has its own distinctive flavor. The rind, having a sharp flavor, is fine for marmalade. It is this fruit that is much in demand for the Scotch marmalades that are so famous.

SCOTCH ORANGE MARMALADE

Pare *naranjas* very thin and with scissors cut into small strips. Put the pulp and juice into kettle with water to just cover. Press down with wooden spoon and strain. To each pint of liquid, put a pound of sugar and the chipped rind. Honey may be substituted for sugar if desired.

ORANGE BRANDY

Rind of 8 oranges ½ gallon French brandy
¾ pint orange juice 1¼ pounds sugar

Cut the orange rinds fine, add to juice and best French brandy letting stand four days. Add sugar, let stand twenty-four hours, strain and cork.

PRESERVED ORANGE FLOWERS

Catch the blossoms on a sheet, pour over them a boiling syrup. Let stand overnight and bring to boiling point the next day; spread on platters or trays, put a sheet of glass over them and let them dry in the sun half a day, then sprinkle well with powdered sugar. Pack in jars. Or they may be sealed hot in syrup. They are very delicate for flavoring drinks, desserts and cakes.

NARANJA DULCE

Peel a naranja and cut in quarters, carefully removing seeds. Boil and throw off this water. Then put the quarters of the naranjas in a syrup made by adding a pound of sugar, enough water to cover the fruit, a stick of cinnamon, and cook on a slow fire. The first water must be thrown off to get rid of the bitterness.

KUMQUATS OR CUMQUATS
(Citrus Japonica)

Resembling miniature oranges, the smallest citrus fruit in cultivation in this country comes into our northern markets, packed in quart boxes with a bit of foliage attached, for the holiday and winter trade.

The kumquat is native of China, where it is called "Gold Orange", or "Kumquat", and also Japan, termed "Kin Kan". In China kumquats are preserved whole, packed in small jars for exportation, forming quite an industry.

The plant grows to be quite a bush of from six to twelve feet in height, and has bright, glossy, dark green leaves, which together with the bright, golden fruit, make a charming combination. The flowers, a trifle smaller than the orange blossoms, are also of the same fragrance. As an ornamental shrub it cannot be surpassed by any other evergreen.

Kumquats are largely used for table decorations. They make a delightful bit of color, halved, by themselves, or with other small fruits, to decorate the punch bowl or salad. They are also very attractive crystallized. In using the fruit, either cooked or fresh, the rind is edible and left intact. They make very delicious marmalade jelly.

KUMQUAT PRESERVES

Clean kumquats thoroughly by washing with pure soap and water. After rinsing in clear water sprinkle with soda, using one tablespoonful of soda to one quart of kumquats, then pour sufficient boiling water over this to cover fruit; let stand ten minutes, pour off water and rinse again; make a slit in each kumquat and place in kettle with sufficient water to cover, boil ten minutes, drain and drop the fruit in a sugar solution made by adding one cup of sugar to one pint of water. Boil slowly until transparent and the syrup is slightly jellied. Pack kumquats in jars and pour the hot syrup over; partly seal and immerse cans in hot water for a few minutes, then screw down tops tightly. Pint jars are best for kumquats.

KUMQUAT MARMALADE

Weigh the fruit and separate the pulp from the skin. Cut the pulp into small pieces and cover with water. Cook thirty minutes. Strain and add one cup of water for each pound of fruit. Cook the skins in water until they are tender, pouring off the water two or three times, if the flavor seems too strong, as many think it is. Drain the skins and put them through a meat-chopper or cut them into slices. Combine juice and peel and add three-fourths of a cup of sugar for each cup of the juice before the skin is added. Boil until it jellies.

CRYSTALLIZED KUMQUATS

Prepare kumquats as in Kumquat Preserves. Drop into boiling water and let boil slowly ten minutes. Change from boiling water to a boiling sugar solution, made by dissolving one-half a cup in one cup of boiling water. Boil for thirty minutes; remove from the sugar solution and place on a platter to dry.

KUMQUAT JELLY

¼ box kumquats   ¼ cup lemon juice
½ cup sugar   1 tablespoon gelatine

Cut one-fourth of a box kumquats in slices, add water to cover, and let simmer slowly one hour; strain, add one-half cup of sugar and one-fourth of a cup of lemon juice. Soak one tablespoonful of gelatine in two tablespoonfuls of cold water and add to the first mixture while hot. Strain, turn into the mould and chill. Garnish with slices of kumquats cooked until soft and rolled in granulated sugar.

KUMQUAT GELATINE

Make lemon Jello, adding kumquats sliced very thin. Serve very cold with cream.

GRAPEFRUIT

Cut the fruit in half, or cut the top off. With a slender grapefruit knife, loosen each section free from the "rag"—remove the core and seeds. Serve ice-cold with a sharp-pointed spoon. In the North, where grapefruit is sometimes shipped green, sugar may be added but fruit ripened on the tree needs no sugar. Puerto Rican grapefruit is especially juicy and sweet.

GRAPEFRUIT CUP

Take out the grapefruit sections or "hearts", add a tablespoon each of marachino and brandy. Garnish with mint leaves. Serve in glasses set in bowls containing shaved ice.

CRYSTALLIZED GRAPEFRUIT PEEL

Use fruit with thick peel. Scrub fruit and cut into quarters; remove the peel and cut it into even srips. For each pound of peel add one quart of cold water and let boil twenty minutes. Pour water off and repeat three times or until all bitter flavor is removed. Drain and while wet add a cup of sugar for each cup of peel; let simmer until all the sugar is absorbed. No more water will be needed, if sugar is added when peel is wet. While hot, roll each piece in sugar and lay on platter to dry.

GRAPEFRUIT SALAD

Use grapefruit hearts on a lettuce leaf with French dressing.

GRAPEFRUIT AND GRAPES

Combine grapefruit hearts with seeded white grapes. Serve on lettuce with either French dressing or mayonnaise.

GRAPEFRUIT-BAR-LE-DUC

Serve halved grapefruit with the centers filled with Bar-le-duc.

GRAPEFRUIT AND ORANGE MARMALADE

Take one grapefruit, one orange and one lemon, cut each into quarters, then slice quarters very thin, through pulp and rind, discarding all the seeds. Weigh this, and to each pound add three pints of cold water and set aside for twenty-four hours. Next day let the fruit boil gently until fruit is very tender.

While hot, weigh this, and to each pound add one pound of sugar and set aside for another twenty-four hours; then cook, stirring to keep from burning until it jellies; it will be a slight amber in color. Store in sterilized glasses like jelly and seal with paraffin.

For grapefruit marmalade, use one lemon to two grapefruits and prepare same as grapefruit and orange marmalade.

Orange marmalade may be made by using three oranges to one lemon.

THE GUAVA
(Psidium Quajava)

Gonzalo de Oviedo in 1526 wrote a *Natural History of the Indies.* In it he says "The guayaba is a handsome tree with leaves like that of the mulberry, but smaller, and the flowers are fragrant; it bears an apple more substantial than those of Spain;—and I have seen the best ones in the Isthmus of Darien and nearby on the mainland, and persons accustomed to it esteem it as a very good fruit, much better than the apple."

The guava is a native of tropical America. It is not very attractive but planting in hedges improves its appearance. The guava contains 4 to 10 percent of sugar and 1 percent of protein. It makes the most delicious of jellies and jam.

UNCOOKED GUAVA

Select ripe perfect fruit, peel, cut in half and remove seeds. Fill the halves with chopped almonds or cashew nuts, grated coconut or whipped cream. Serve as dessert.

STEWED GUAVA

Cut in half, remove seeds. Cover with water and simmer until tender. Then add sugar to taste and cool.

GUAVA SALAD

Peel and slice fruit, remove seeds. Serve on lettuce with cooked dressing or mayonnaise.

GUAVA CHUTNEY

5 pounds guavas	1 tablespoon ginger
2 pounds brown sugar	1 tablespoon mustard
2 quarts vinegar	4 tablespoons salt
2 pounds chopped seedless raisins	Tumeric to taste
1 minced clove of garlic	2 chopped pepper pods

Peel and quarter the guavas, cook and strain, or the fruit may be left in pieces, removing the seeds. To five pounds of fruit add two pounds brown sugar, two quarts of vinegar. Simmer until tender and then add chopped seedless raisins and garlic and cook a few minutes. Then add ginger, mustard, salt, a little tumeric, and chopped pepper pods. Let stand overnight, in the morning stir well, heat to boiling, pack in sterilized jars while boiling hot and seal.

GUAVA BROWN BETTY

Follow recipe for Gooseberry Brown Betty.

GUAVA JELLY

Cut guavas in quarters, cover with water and boil thoroughly. Take off and strain in a jelly bag. To a pint of juice add a pint of sugar. Let boil half an hour before sugar is added. Let boil three times, skim, pour into glasses, hot.

GUAVA PASTE

Prepare as for jelly but mash the fruit after it is cooked. Strain and cook again in a double-boiler. Prepare a syrup separately with three-fourths cup sugar to one cup fruit pulp, put together and cook until it forms a ball when dropped into cold water. Pour into boxes that are lined with waxed or oiled paper.

FROZEN GUAVA

Cook guavas until tender and mash. Strain to remove seeds. To a pound of fruit add a pound of sugar and a pint of water, juice and grated rind of a small lime. Mix well and freeze.

THE MAMEY or Mammaee Apple
(*Mammea Americana*)

The Mamey belongs to the family *Clusiaceæ*. It is a handsome tree with large glossy leaves, and its graceful erect habit of growth makes it conspicuous on the landscape; it is indigenous to tropical America and is sometimes called "Santo Domingo Apricot". The fruit grows to the size of a grapefruit, rich in color and with an aromatic smell; it has a brown skin. Christopher Columbus described the Mamey as a fruit the size of a large lemon, with the flavor of a peach. In Central America the seed is ground with cacao in making chocolate. The wood of the tree is valued for timber as it is durable and beautifully grained. From its gum is made an incense. The pulp is juicy and firm and its flavor is not unlike the quince. The fragrant white flowers yield by distillation an essential oil used in liqueurs under the name of "Eau de Creole". The ripe fruit may be eaten raw, but never use milk at the same meal.

It was this fruit that kept Cortez and his army alive on their famous march from Mexico City to Honduras.

SLICED MAMEY

Slice the fruit thin, sprinkle with powdered sugar or wine and sugar.

PRESERVED MAMEY

Slice into chips, drop into syrup, boil with a bit of stick cinnamon and slice of a lime.

MAMEY BUTTER

Prepare as for preserves, mash through a sieve and seal hot into jars.

MAMEY PUDDING

Slice the fruit, put in a baking dish with alternate layers of brown sugar, bread-crumbs (or grapenuts) until dish is full. Dot with butter and bake in a moderate oven until done. Serve warm with a lemon sauce.

MAMEY SHERBET

Slice the fruit, stew in a syrup, add the juice of a lime, strain and freeze, adding two teaspoonfuls of gelatine dissolved in water.

MAMEY AND PINEAPPLE DULCE

To two mameys peeled and cut in small slices, add the juice of one pineapple and enough water to cover. Add one and one-half cups sugar and boil until the fruit is tender when it may be sealed in glass jars as other preserves.

MAMEY AND GOOSEBERRY JELLY

Slice, cook and mash the fruit. To one pint of juice add one pint of sugar. Let juice boil half an hour before sugar is added and have the sugar heated. Cook until it strings and seal hot.

MANGO
(Anacardiaceæ)

The mango tree would be grown for its dense shade and the beauty of its glossy foliage alone. The fruit is a drupe. It came originally from the Himalaya country from where it has been carried to all tropical countries. The timber, though soft, serves for common purposes: combined with sandalwood it was used in cremation by the ancients. In the thirteenth century a Persian poet wrote:

> "The Mango is the pride of the garden,
> The choicest fruit of Hindustan,
> Other fruits we are content to eat when ripe
> But the mango is good in all stages of growth."

Other writers have lavished praise on the fruit. Fryer, in 1673, said: "The Apples of the Hesperides are but Fables to them." It is said to be a fruit cultivated upwards of 4,000 years. A Chinese traveler, Hwen T'sang, visited Hindustan in the year 632 A.D. and carried the mango to the outside world. Friar Jordanus who visited the East in 1328 wrote of the mango: "There is another tree which bears a fruit the size of plum, sweet and pleasant."

The Portuguese are thought to have brought the mango to tropical

America, and the tree is known to have been introduced into Barbadoes in 1742. No doubt early Spanish galleons brought it to Puerto Rico.

It has been said that the proper place to eat ripe "mangoes" is in the bathtub on account of the juice and pulp spreading over one's countenance. This is true of the poorer varieties but the finer ones are as manageable as peaches or other fruits.

Green, the fruit is used for pickles and preserves: ripe, for desserts either raw or cooked. The kernels of the seeds are sometimes roasted and eaten like chestnuts.

MANGO CHIPS

8 pounds mango chips	4 lemons
4 pounds sugar	¼ pound ginger root

Cut lemons in small pieces, mix all ingredients and cook down slowly.

MANGO HONEY

Run mangoes through the food-chopper. Add enough water to keep pulp from burning, and three-fourths the weight in sugar. Cook slowly. Turn out into glasses.

MANGO SAUCE

Choose green mangoes about one or two weeks before ripe. Cut from seeds; boil until soft; sweeten to taste. This is a very good substitute for apples in sauce, pies or puddings.

MANGO JAM

Peel and slice mangoes and boil ten minutes in water. Make a syrup with sugar and the water in which mangoes were cooked. Put mangoes in syrup and cook again until quite thick. Proportions of sugar to mangoes are to taste.

MANGOES FROZEN

1 dozen mangoes	1 lemon
1 large cup sugar	3 egg-whites

For a dozen mangoes use a large cup of sugar and a pint of water. Press the ripe fruit through a sieve and let stand to dissolve the sugar. Add juice of a lemon and bit of the grated rind. Then add the well-beaten whites of three eggs and freeze.

MANGO SHERBET

1 quart mangoes	½ pound sugar
1 lemon	3 egg-whites

Boil the sugar and one quart water together for five minutes. Press the mangoes through a sieve, add the lemon juice, and when cold freeze the same as ice cream, then add the meringue.

Mamey sherbet is made in precisely the same manner.

SLICED MANGOES

Slice nice ripe mangoes, squeeze a bit of fresh lime juice on them.

MANGO PIE

Prepare pastry for pie crust, proceed as for apple pie, using either green or ripe mangoes, add sugar, lemon juice (or lime) with a bit of the grated skin, a dash of cinnamon. Cover with crust or with strips of pastry and bake.

MANGO SLUMP—1

Make a rich baking powder biscuit dough. Roll very thin and lay in baking tin. Cover with chopped ripe mangoes, sprinkle over these sugar and ground cinnamon, dot with butter. Bake from one-half to three-quarters of an hour and serve with any sweet.

MANGO SLUMP—2

Stew six good-sized green mangoes until soft, sweeten a little but not enough for eating. Make a biscuit crust and drop this onto the fruit while it is boiling hot. Bake in a hot oven and serve with a hard sauce.

MANGO BROWN BETTY

Stew green mangoes until soft. Put a layer in the bottom of the baking dish. Cover with a thick layer of bread-crumbs. Sprinkle thickly with sugar and cinnamon; do this until the baking dish is full. Dot the top with pieces of butter. Bake closely covered for forty minutes. Remove the cover and brown. Serve with hard sauce.

MANGO BUTTER

Run mangoes (green) through food-chopper. To one pint fruit add two pints water and two and a half pints sugar. Boil down thick. Seal like jelly.

BAKED MANGOES

Slice ripe mangoes in a baking dish, using sugar generously if the fruit is tart. Add bits of butter and a cup of hot water; sprinkle with chopped nuts and bake until tender. Serve cold with a lemon sauce.

PICKLED MANGOES

Spice-bag: 1 tablespoon each:

Powdered cinnamon	1 cup vinegar
Cloves	½ cup sugar
Allspice	Mangoes
Mace	

Pare and cut the mangoes into small pieces. In a small cloth bag put a tablepoonful each of powdered cinnamon, cloves, allspice and a little mace, put it in a kettle with a cup of vinegar, heat it slowly to boiling point, then remove the spice-bag, add sugar, and when hot put in the mangoes, and the spice-bag again. Cook until the mangoes are tender and seal while boiling hot, in glass jars.

MANGO SALAD

¾ cup cooked rice	3 mangoes, sliced
Lettuce	Red and green pepper

Indian Dressing

Pare and slice the mangoes, mix lightly with the rice. Chill. Serve on crisp leaves of lettuce and garnish with chopped red and green pepper. Serve with Indian Dressing.

INDIAN DRESSING

½ cup French dressing	2 teaspoons chopped hard-cooked egg
½ teaspoon curry powder	Salt and pepper

Place, in a covered jar, the French dressing, chopped hard-cooked eggs and seasoning. Shake well until thoroughly blended. Chill and serve.

PINEAPPLE OR PIÑA

(Ananassa Ananas)

The pineapple is a fruit for which Puerto Rico has long been famous, a variety known in northern markets as "Porto Ricans".

The custom so prevalent in Puerto Rico of placing the sliced fruit in salt water before eating is evidently very old, as Acosta says of the inhabitants of the West Indies, "they eat it being cut in morsels and steeped a while in water and salt." There is also a belief, more or less widespread, in Puerto Rico, that pineapple and coffee should not be partaken of at the same meal. No doubt the ferment which it contains might affect certain combinations of food. The active principle of the fruit is ananasine, since an early writer speaks of it as a "digestant" active with "either acids or alkaline carbonates". The juice is healing in catarrhal affections and it is recommended for ordinary sore throat. The pineapple is generally conceded to be one of the finest fruits in existence and is indigenous to tropical America, but has been greatly improved by cultivation.

The stem and stump of pineapple are rich in starch but in the fruit itself there is none.

The beauty of pineapple is in its shape and color, which is lost if it is peeled and cut up. Cut the pineapple in wedge-shaped pieces passing the knife from crown to base, the middle being left just entire enough to hold in place until time for serving; the wedges can then be easily dislodged with a thin knife and fork. Another way is to cut the pineapple in horizontal slices with a very sharp knife, the slices kept together and the crown left on; the pineapple can then be passed whole, in the center of a dish of assorted fruits.

Pineapple can be grated or sliced after being peeled. A ripe fresh pineapple needs no sugar, for it changes the delicate flavor. Grated pineapple with a glass of sherry poured over it and served very cold is delicious.

PINEAPPLE SYRUP

Cut the pineapple in small pieces and to each three pounds add one quart of water, boil until soft. Mash and strain into another vessel and to each pint of juice syrup add from three-fourths to one pound of white sugar. Boil to a rich syrup, bottle and seal air-tight.

FROZEN PINEAPPLE AND MARSHMALLOW SALAD

1 cup whipping cream	1 slice pineapple, quartered
½ cup mayonnaise	12 marshmallows
3¾ cups diced, canned pineapple, drained	1 cup shredded coconut

Whip the cream and fold in the mayonnaise. Combine the diced pineapple, marshmallows, and coconut, and fold into the mayonnaise mixture. Freeze in the tray of an automatic refrigerator. Unmold on a platter of crisp lettuce and garnish with pineapple slices, quartered.

PINEAPPLE BISQUE

3 cups grated pineapple	1 tablespoon caramel
1 cup sugar (or less)	5 teaspoons sherry flavoring
1 cup cream.	½ pound macaroon-crumbs
1 cup whipping cream	

Use grated fresh or thoroughly drained canned crushed pineapple, in this recipe. If canned is used, cut amount of sugar in half.

Cook grated pineapple with sugar until it is thick, about fifteen minutes. Heat one cup of cream in a double boiler. Add caramel and stir until it is thoroughly combined. When it is hot, but not boiling, combine with pineapple mixture, stirring constantly. Cool. Whip another cup of cream until it thickens and begins to hold its shape, then fold it with sherry flavoring into the cool mixture and pour into freezing trays. Place in freezing compartment of refrigerator. When it is frozen to a mush, stir well and fold in macaroon-crumbs. Complete freezing.

PINEAPPLE TAPIOCA PUDDING

Cook tapioca slowly in salted water until done so that it will pour easily. Have as much pineapple as preferred cut in cubes in a dish, cover the pineapple with a little sugar, pour the hot tapioca over the pineapple, stir all together and cool. To be eaten with whipped cream or a thin custard.

DULCE DE PIÑA

Peel a pineapple and cut into small pieces or leave in slices. Add enough water to cover, and for a pound of fruit a pound of sugar. When the fruit is tender seal as for preserves.

POMARROSA

(Eugenia Jambos)

The rose-apple or pomarrosa also belongs to the myrtle family, of the genus Eugenia. Originally from the East Indies it has become naturalized in the West Indies and has been carried to all parts of the tropics. In India where it is abundant, it is called Rosejaman or gulab-jaman.

Pomarrosa is esteemed as an ornamental. The fresh fruit is attractive and fragrant but is not usually eaten raw. In jelly or preserves it is delicious. Often it is used as table decoration on account of its beauty. The enticing fragrance is not unlike rose water.

SLICED POMARROSA

For dessert peel and slice, serve with wine and sugar.

STEWED POMARROSA

Peel and slice, simmer gently with enough water to cover and a pound of sugar for each pound of fruit.

POMARROSA PRESERVES

Prepare a syrup, with sugar pound for pound, drop the pomarrosa whole (that is with the top and seeds removed) into the syrup, cook fifteen minutes and seal boiling hot in glass jars.

POMEGRANATE
(Punica Granatum)

The pomegranate is found in Africa and Asia. Like the acanthus leaf it was used as a motif in ancient design. The bark and rind of the fruit contain yellow dye used to color leather in Morocco. The rind, flowers and root are astringent and used medicinally in many countries.

"Eat the pomegranate," said a prophet of Moslem, "for it purges the system of envy and hatred." King Solomon had a hedge of pomegranate bushes and the Children of Israel mourned in their exile saying, "it is no place of seed, or of fig or of vine or of pomegranates." The pomegranate, with its mystic origin and early sacred associations, was long reverenced by the Persians and Jews, an old tradition having identified it as the forbidden fruit given to Adam by Eve. It is a common fruit all over tropical countries.

The bush resembles Japan quince and has showy red flowers. There is little demand for the fruit in the general market, but one occasionally comes across it. The seeds are surrounded by a pulp which makes beautiful jelly. Care should be taken when passing the seeds through a colander to remove the pulp from the seeds not to bruise the seeds for if broken an unpleasant flavor results. The uncooked juice is cooling in fevers. With sugar added and boiled it makes a good syrup, which if frozen is a delicious ice.

POMEGRANATE ICE

Cut ripe fruit in half and remove the pulp from the seeds with care. To a pint of juice add a pint of sugar, dissolve, stirring well, strain, and freeze.

POMEGRANATE SYRUP

Ten parts of fruit pulp and eleven of sugar, mix and let stand twenty-four hours. Then put on to boil up once, strain immediately. This liquid is excellent to sweeten drinks, being refreshing and somewhat astringent at the same time.

ROSELLE
RED SORREL OF GUINEA
(Aleluja de Guinea, Hibiscus Sabdariffa)

The sorrel or roselle is a fine jelly-maker. It bears fruit in the cool season, then dies, when the seeds must be replanted. The calyx is bright red and picked apart and heated it makes a bright red juice which rivals the currant in flavor. Only the calyx is used. Use about three-fourths of a pound of sugar to a pint of juice for jelly. The flowers may also be used to make pies or tarts or boiled down whole into a preserve. The flower is somewhat like cranberry but more delicate, and deserves to be more generally known.

Where neither red currant nor cranberries grow, it offers a pleasant substitute for jellies or sauce. A cooling summer drink is made from an infusion of the calyx, its natural bright color giving a very attractive quality to the drink. It may be bottled hot with no sugar, and kept for use during the part of the year it is not bearing.

ROSELLE JELLY
(MRS. WALTERS)

Pick off the calyx, cover with water, cook down and strain in a jelly-bag. To a pound of juice use three-fourths as much of sugar. Boil up three times, skim and fill jelly glasses. The glasses should be wrapped in paper as the jelly fades in a strong light.

ROSELLE SYRUP

Proceed as for jelly, use more water and bottle hot. Dilute with ice-water when serving.

ROSELLE PRESERVES

Pick the calyx apart, cover with water, add three-fourths pound sugar to each pound of fruit. Do not strain but bottle as it is, after it has cooked until soft and clear.

ROSELLE TAPIOCA

3 tablespoons tapioca
1 cup sweetened roselle juice
¼ cup orange juice
1 teaspoon grated orange rind
Cream or top milk

To one cup boiling water add tapioca and cook in double boiler twenty minutes. Stir occasionally. Remove from the fire, add sweetened roselle juice, orange juice and rind. Chill and serve with cream or top milk.

ROSELLE PIE

Pick off the petals and use as fruit would be used with sugar for a pie filling.

SEAGRAPE
(Coccolaba uvifera)

The seagrape or shoregrape, so common in Puerto Rico, the broad-leaved plant growing all along our beaches, has bunches of grape-like fruits, purple red when ripe. They make excellent jelly or marmalade.

They are used in gastro-intestinal disorders and to make a syrup for coughs. It is said the Caribs used their large leaves for plates, and early explorers found that the leaves when worn in their hats warded off the fevers caused by too much sun. When lettuce is not in season, the seagrape leaves make a substitute as a garnish, although not edible. They are attractive to use in serving melon or papaya, too.

TAMARINDUS INDICA

To primitive man the world in general is animate, he thinks trees and plants have souls like his own and he treats them accordingly. Tree spirits were thought to give rain and sunshine, to make the crops to grow. In order to get rain in Burma, the largest tamarind tree was chosen to receive bread, coconut, plantains and fowls, given by the people to the spirit of rain, the "nat", and they prayed, "Oh, Lord Nat, have pity on us mortals and stay not the rain."

The tamarind tree is one of our most beautiful trees, with wide spreading branches and delicate fine leaves. It has small pink and white flowers which develop into long edible pods with a crust-like skin. Removing this skin or shell, each seed will be found to have a thick pulpy covering, which has a pleasant sour taste. The fruit has been known to commerce since Marco Polo mentioned it in 1298. The origin of the name is Arabic, tamar-u-l-Hind, meaning "date of India". It was known in India, Arabia and Africa. New England sea-captains sailing to the West Indies in the eighteenth and nineteenth centuries brought the preserved fruit to New England and found the acid and sugar content of the fruit valuable to seamen to offset the starchy diet. The fruit is refrigerant and laxative. It is said that a tree bears 350 pounds of fruit in a year. It contains both citric and tartaric acid. Made into cooling drinks it has a laxative effect on the system, of much value in illness and in the prevention of it. Like many tropical trees it has a number of useful attributes: the pulp may be used in rheumatism; the pods powdered provide a strong glue; the leaves are useful in jaundice and as poultice for sore eyes or ulcers; from a decoction of the bark is provided a yellow dye; it is useful in curing asthma; the timber is valuable for building. It is said that no one should sleep in the shade of the tamarind, due to an acid exhalation it gives off, and it is true that the cloth of tents pitched under them has been rapidly affected.

Tamarinds are much used in the preparation of curries.

TAMARIND MARMALADE

Put tamarinds over a slow fire with enough water to cover. Wash the pulp from the seeds through a colander, add sugar pound for pound.

TAMARIND SYRUP

To make syrup, add twice the quantity of water and bottle hot. For cooling drinks add cracked ice and a half glass water to the quantity of this syrup. It is a delicious summer drink.

TAMARIND CHUTNEY (Malay Recipe)

1 pound dates	½ pound green ginger root
1 pound large raisins	¼ pound brown sugar
½ pound tamarinds	2 tablespoons salt
4 large onions	1 cup tarragon vinegar
4 green peppers	

Remove stones from one pound of dates, and chop with one pound large raisins and half pound tamarinds. Grind together onions, green peppers, and green ginger root that has been scraped and sliced. Add brown sugar, salt, and tarragon vinegar. Mix all well together, heat to boiling point and then seal in glass jars.

Green mangoes cut up may be substituted for the dates.

BERRIES

THE FRESA
(Rubus Rosaefolious)

Fresa is said to come from the French word for raspberry—*framboesa*. A story tells of the seeds having been brought accidentally in the saddle-bags of a Spanish traveller in the Himalayas, and thence to Puerto Rico.

Certain it is that the West Indias is the only place in this part of the world where it is recorded and one may well believe that it has escaped from its first cultivation and scattered itself over the mountain sides. Not quite so luscious in texture as its relative, the raspberry, neverthless it has its own delicate, delightful flavor.

FRESH FRESA BERRIES

Wash carefully in a colander, then scatter powdered sugar over them and set them in the ice-box to chill. Serve with cream or top-milk.

FRESA SHORTCAKE

Prepare individual baking powder biscuits. Mash berries with some sugar, split the biscuits, butter, and put the mashed berries on the lower half of the biscuit. Place the upper half of the biscuit on top, on this put some fresh uncrushed berries and serve with whipped cream.

FRESA WINE

4 quarts berries	1 pound sugar
1 quart cider vinegar	1 pint brandy

Mash berries and sugar in vinegar and let stand in sun half a day; strain, add a pint of brandy; bottle, seal and out away in a cool place.

FRESA JAM

To a pound of fruit add a pound of sugar and half a pound of grosellas that have been cooked and strained. Simmer together twenty minutes and seal hot.

FRESA ICE

Mash one pound of fresas, cover with sugar, heat well. Strain and squeeze. Just before freezing add the whites of two eggs, well-beaten.

FRESA ICE CREAM

1 pound fresas	1 can evaporated milk
½ pound sugar	1 quart milk
3 egg yolks	1 teaspoon arrowroot
Vanilla or lime juice	

Add sugar to fresas; mash and strain. Make a custard with egg yolks, milk, and evaporated milk, and one teaspoon arrowroot. When cold add to the fresas. Add more sugar and a dash of vanilla or lime, if desired. Freeze.

FRESA JELLY

Cover with water, boil, strain through a jelly-bag. Add sugar pint for pint, boil. Let boil up three times, skim and put in jelly glasses.

FRESA VINEGAR

Cover any quantity of fresas with vinegar and let stand overnight, squeeze through a cheesecloth, add a pint of sugar to a pint of juice and boil well. Skim clean and seal while boiling hot in bottles.

GOOSEBERRY
(Cicca Disticha)

The Spanish "Gooseberry" is really not a gooseberry at all but *cicca disticha*, white waxy berries growing in clusters on a tree which is very ornamental with its composite leaves of soft green. The children love its puckery taste and when the tree is full of fruit it is usually full of small boys. It is also called "cherry". In olden times the decoction of the leaves was considerably used in treating yellow fever.

GOOSEBERRY OR GROSELLA PRESERVES

To a pound of berries add enough water to cover, if after a time this water is thrown off the fruit will be less acid. Put on fresh water and one and a half pounds of sugar. Let boil up well and while boiling hot seal in glass jars.

WEST INDIAN GOOSEBERRY PUDDING

3 cups gooseberries
Flour for dredging berries
2 eggs
1 tablespoon melted butter

1 pint milk
4 cups prepared flour
Hard sauce

Wash fruit that has been cut from the seeds, dredge with flour, beat light, stir into them melted butter and milk. Then add prepared flour. Last of all stir in the fruit, well-dredged with flour. Turn into a greased mold and steam for three hours. Serve with hard sauce.

WEST INDIAN GOOSEBERRY BROWN BETTY

2 cups of fruit cut from the seeds
1 cup fine bread-crumbs

2 tablespoons of butter
1½ cups of sugar

Butter a bake-dish and put in bottom a layer of fruit. Sprinkle well with sugar and a little cinnamon. Over this spread a layer of crumbs, then add another layer of fruit, and so forth, until dish is full. Dot top layer with butter lumps. Bake closely covered for forty minutes. Remove the cover and brown. Serve hot with hard butter and sugar sauce.

GOOSEBERRY CHUTNEY

4 pounds gooseberries
2 pounds tamarinds
1 pound sugar
½ pound raisins
½ pound ginger

¼ pound garlic
¼ pound mustard seed
1 quart vinegar
¼ pound salt

Four pounds ripe gooseberries, two pounds of tamarinds; one pound of sugar, half a pound of raisins, half a pound of ginger, quarter of a pound of garlic, quarter of a pound of mustard seed. Boil the fruit in a quart of vinegar with the sugar, grind the other ingredients with another bottle of vinegar and quarter of a pound of salt. Mix and boil twenty minutes. Let it cool and then bottle for use.

RED CHERRY

(Malphigia Glabra)

This is a bright red fruit, not properly a cherry, but commonly called so: it contains three seeds. Any recipe for gooseberries can be followed, with perhaps using a little less sugar as it is not such a tart fruit.

MULTA OR MURTA BERRIES
(*Myrciaria* or Myrtle Family)

"Las murtas son como ojos
negros de nuestras mujeres,
las guindas, sus albios rojos,
guindas son nuestros antojos,
murtas, son nuestros quereres."

Murtas are like the dark eyes
of our women,
like cherries are our whims,
murtas are our desires.

—*"Las Frutas Borinqueñas" by Conrado Asenjo.*

Murta is a wild fruit tree of the genus Eugenia. The wood is used for making charcoal. The berries are not unlike the gooseberry in flavor. In Vieques they are used for coloring rum. Rich in flavor and coloring, the syrup can be used for cordials, pudding sauces, desserts and drinks. The murta is widely cultivated and prized in Brazil. There are many closely allied varieties.

MURTA SYRUP

Cook berries until soft, mash and strain. To a pint of juice add a pint of sugar, cook until clear and bottle. To serve dilute with ice-water.

MURTA CORDIAL

1 quart murta juice	1 tablespoon cloves
1 pound sugar	1 tablespoon cinnamon
1 cup rum or brandy	1 tablespoon nutmeg

To one quart of juice add granulated sugar, one tablespoon each of cloves, cinnamon, and nutmeg; boil fifteen minutes. Add a cupful rum or brandy, bottle while hot.

NISPERO OR SAPODILLA
(*Achras Sapota*)

The tree belonging to the family Sapotaceæ is commonly cultivated in Puerto Rico, being a very beautiful shade tree with shiny dark leaves. A synonym of this is the *ausubo*, distinguished for its beautiful wood. The Nispero wood is strong and hard.

Lintels supposed to be made of this wood are found in ruins of Tikal (Central America) dated according to Mayan chronology of about 470 A.D. The wood is resistant to the hurricanes of tropical America.

In recent years it has been cultivated in Mexico for the "gum chicle" it yields, which can be used in manufacturing chewing-gum. The fruit looks not unlike an Irish potato, small and brown, and should be served very cold, quartered.

OTAHEITE—JAMAICA PLUM
(*Spondias Lutea*)

The Otaheite plum, Jamaica plum, or hog plum, is related to the Otaheite apple, but its fruit resembles the loquat somewhat. Its pulp can be made into marmalade or mashed with sugar into a syrup for drinks. The tree itself is ornamental, growing into spreading Japanesy shapes.

THE TROPICAL PAPAW
(*Carica Papaya*)

This beautiful and luscious fruit is commonly called "lechosa" or "papaya lechosa". The tree resembles a palm and the fruit hangs close to the trunk, shaded by large, graceful, curiously cut leaves. It is not unlike a melon, and the ripe fruit is served like a melon, with salt or lime juice. In stomach trouble it is especially nourishing, containing as it does a vegetable pepsin. The leaves have a singular effect upon meat. If tough meat is wrapped in the leaves and left in the ice-box a few hours it will be found to have become surprisingly tender.

The poet Walter wrote in 1635 of the Carica Papaya:

> "*The Palma Christi and the fair Papaw.*
> *Now but a seed (preventing Nature's Law)*
> *In half the circle of the hasty year*
> *Project a shade, and lovely fruits do bear.*"

"There is also a fruite," wrote a traveler in 1598, "that came out of the Spanish Indies, it is called Papaois and is very like a Mellon and will not grow, but always two together, that is male and female and when they are divided and set apart, then they yield no fruits at all."

The ripe fruit may be cut into sections and served like melon with lime juice or it may be cut up and served as a fruit cocktail. It is perhaps best with lemon or lime juice.

The green fruit stewed is not unlike summer squash and should be served as a vegetable.

DULCE DE PAPAYA

1 papaya	1 stick cinnamon
1 cup sugar	1 clove
Juice and grated rind of ½ lemon	

Peel the fruit in squares, put on to cook with a little water. Add sugar and the juice and grated rind of half a lemon, a piece of stick cinnamon and one clove to flavor. Cook until soft. Serve cold as a dessert.

CRYSTALLIZED GREEN PAPAYA

Drop squares of green papaya into syrup and boil until it candies; it may be flavored with mint or wintergreen.

LECHOSA OR GREEN PAPAYA PRESERVES

1 lechosa	1 lime
2 cups sugar	1 stick cinnamon

Peel a lechosa, remove seeds and cut in small pieces. Prepare a syrup with sugar, add peel and juice of a lime, a stick of cinnamon, three cups of water. Cook until the fruit is transparent and seal hot.

VANILLA AND GINGER

VANILLA PLANIFOLIA

THE vanilla is one of the important spice plants indigenous to tropical America; the Aztecs used it long before the Spaniards came to Mexico. The earliest botanical notice is given in 1605 by the apothecary to Queen Elizabeth. The Spaniards carried it over the world and nowhere in the world has it been possible to equal the vanilla of the Western Hemisphere. It is a large clinging orchid with waxy leaves and racemes of pale green flowers, the elongated stem climbs by means of tendril-like roots. The vanilla, surrounded by the beautiful and idle catalaya and other highly colored orchids, that "toil not, neither do they spin" seems content to fulfill its humble mission, and literally "keeps its feet on the ground" for, while it is an epiphyte it has its roots in the ground unlike other orchids, and produces one of the most important contributions to the diet of man.

The vanilla blossom would not be converted into a pod unless it were polonized by hand, by man or by the Mexican Wasp-bee. The polonization done by hand is very easy, done generally by girls, pushing the pollen into the cup or pistil by the aid of a wooden needle. The wasp-bee having a small body and back legs, when extracting the honey only pushes the pollen and makes the polonization. The best cured vanilla pods are the Mexican, receiving a price of $6.00 and $7.00 a pound, Guadalupe vanilla (French island of the Antilles), the price fetching $4.00 a pound is only polonized by hand. The Puerto Rican vanilla in Adjuntas and Utuado grows alongside the River of Arecibo, between Utuado and Adjuntas, is also pollonized by hand. The tree on which the vine grows and takes shelter is the "bucayo enano", the most leguminous tree in existence. This plant requires from 110 to 120 inches of rain a year.

Planting the vanilla in Puerrto Rico, under the "bucayo enano" would assure, within five years, a stable industry for Puerto Rico, and would give occupation to tens of thousands of families during the polonization, which is practically the whole year round.

Certainly vanilla seems the only economic product from the tremendous genera of orchids. The fruit is a pod from six to ten inches long, the beans of which are used to extract the flavor. They can be pounded in a mortar and used to flavor as well as made into liquid extract. The old sailing vessels in the early times used to carry them to New England in the bean.

TO MAKE EXTRACT OF VANILLA

Pound 1 pound vanilla beans in a mortar and add one gallon of proof spirits (not alcohol). Let stand five or six weeks shaking it occasionally. Strain off as wanted.

GINGER

No root is more delightful than *Zingiber officianalis* or ginger plant or put to greater variety of uses. Originally from Africa it was brought into the West Indies at an early day and soon became an article of commerce.

Interested in developing agriculture, it is said that Ponce de Léon deserves credit for introducing ginger which for many years was a most profitable crop for the island.

The roots are dug when about a year old, cleaned and scalded and dried for shipping. Young tender roots are used for preserves. There also grows here the Shell Lily, *Alpinia nutans,* a member of the same botanical family, which may be preserved with similar results.

PRESERVED GINGER

Scrape young roots, weigh, and allow equal weight of sugar. Boil roots and sugar separately, allowing one-half teaspoon cream of tartar, a half pint of water to each pound of sugar for the syrup. Skim the syrup and when the ginger roots can be easily pierced put them into the syrup, boil up well and seal in jars. One may add the juice of a lemon and the grated rind of one, to every three pounds of ginger, to vary the flavor.

GINGER

Scrape the outside from the green ginger, and boil it in a little water till it is soft; then take it out, and scrape off any spots that are on it; make a syrup of half a pint of sugar and a pound of ginger; let it boil slowly about half an hour; take it up and boil the syrup a little longer.

GINGER WINE (BARBADOES RECIPE)

12 ounces ginger	10 lemons
15 pounds sugar	Yeast

Add bruised ginger to nine gallons of water. Boil a half hour, then add sugar and rind of lemons. Let stand to cool. Then add yeast, following directions for use on the particular kind of yeast you use. Let stand till clear, then close the bung. Bottle and let stand a couple of months.

GINGER EXTRACT

Bruise ginger roots. To one ounce of root add half a cup pure grain alcohol. Stand several days, then strain and bottle.

GINGER NECTAR

1½ pounds sugar	1 lemon
1 egg-white	1 yeast-cake
1 ounce ginger	

In one gallon of water dissolve granulated sugar, add white of one egg beaten and strained, mix together and let come to a boil. Skim clean, add ginger and boil fifteen minutes. When cool add the juice and grated rind of a lemon, one yeast-cake dissolved in a little water, stir well together, bottle and seal air-tight.

GINGER ICE CREAM

½ pound ginger	¼ cup ginger syrup
3 pints thin cream	3 tablespoons sherry wine
1 cup sugar	

Cut ginger in small pieces, mix all ingredients and freeze. Use one part rock salt to three parts finely crushed ice.

GINGER SHERBET

1 pound sugar	1 lemon
5 oranges	½ cup preserved ginger

Boil sugar in one cup of water until it threads. Save out a small amount of syrup and to the rest add juice of the oranges and lemon. Partly freeze. Then add the ginger which has been cut up in small pieces and covered with the syrup saved out. Finish freezing.

GINGERSNAPS

2 cups brown sugar
1 cup butter
1 teaspoon saleratus
½ cup milk or water

1 egg
1 tablespoon ginger, powdered
¾ cup flour

Mix, roll thin, cut with round cookie cutter and bake.

GINGER COOKIES

2 cups molasses
1½ tablespoons powdered ginger
½ cup water
1 teaspoon cinnamon

½ cup butter or lard
½ teaspoon soda
2½ cups flour

These cookies are to be rolled out not too thin, cut with a cookie-cutter; baked on a sheet in a moderate oven.

OLD CHARCOAL STOVE

BREAD

(MARY TERRY)

*"I live with bread like you, feel want,
Taste grief, need friends."—Richard II.*

BANANA BREAD

1 pound butter
2 cups sugar
1 teaspoon vanilla
4 or 5 large eggs
4 or 5 large bananas

4 cups flour
1 teaspoon soda
½ teaspoon baking powder
Pinch of salt

Cream the butter and sugar, add the vanilla, and the eggs, unbeaten, one at a time and beat well after each addition. Sift the flour with the soda and baking powder and salt. Mash the bananas which should be very ripe, with a potato masher, and on them put a teaspoon fresh lime or lemon juice. (Do not use the extract.)

Now add alternately the banana and the flour mixture to the creamed mixture. Begin with the flour to prevent curdling. When all is added, a cup of nut meats may be put in. Stir well and put into two bread tins, and bake in a moderate oven 45 minutes. This bread keeps well.

PLANTAIN FLOUR MUFFINS

2 well-beaten eggs
2 tablespoons sugar
1½ cups sweet milk
3 cups plantain flour

2 teaspoons soda
2 teaspoons cream of tartar
Salt to taste

Beat the above thoroughly and bake in hot gem pans twenty-five minutes.

CORN-MEAL MUFFINS

½ cup corn-meal
1 cup flour
3 teaspoons baking powder
½ teaspoon salt

1 egg
1 tablespoon melted butter
¾ cup mixed evaporated milk
and water

Mix and sift dry ingredients; add milk gradually, egg well-beaten, and melted butter; bake in hot oven in gem pans twenty-five minutes.

ORANGE BISCUITS

2 cups flour
4 teaspoons baking powder
3 tablespoons lard

1 teaspoon salt
¾ to 1 cup milk

Cream the lard, add salt and flour which has been sifted with the baking powder, gradually add the milk for a soft dough, roll out on a floured board. Cut with a small cookie cutter or a small glass and bake in a hot oven.

These may be made very small and served with tea or coffee at an afternoon party.

ORANGE FILLING

2 tablespoons butter
1 tablespoon orange juice

Grated rind 1 orange
4 tablespoons sugar

Cook over moderate heat until thickened a little, then cool. Make baking powder biscuit dough as above, roll out thin. Spread with orange filling, and roll up like a jelly roll. Cut off in half-inch slices, sprinkle with a little sugar and bake in hot oven. Do not have them touch in pan.

CORN FLOUR WAFFLES

2 eggs
1 pint milk
3 cups corn flour

1 teaspoon salt
1 tablespoon melted shortening
2 heaping teaspoons baking powder

To the beaten yolks of the eggs, add milk, or milk and water mixed, corn flour, salt, melted shortening and baking powder. Stir in carefully the whites of eggs, well-beaten, and bake in a hot well-greased waffle-iron for about two minutes.

CILE'S WAFFLES

1 egg
2 tablespoons sugar
2 cups sour milk
¾ teaspoon soda

1½ teaspoons baking powder
3½ cups flour (about)
1 tablespoon melted fat

Beat up the egg in a large bowl, and add sugar and sour milk. Mix soda and baking powder with a little flour and add to the other mixture. Stir in enough flour so that the spoon makes a track which will last for a moment, and then add the melted fat (which may be from the pan of sausage or bacon, which is frying on the stove just as well as not). Have the iron quite hot, and grease both sides with a twist of clean cloth or paper dipped in drippings. Put about two and one-half tablespoonfuls of butter in the middle of the iron, put the cover down, and turn it over immediately. Do not look at it until you are reasonably sure that one side is done, or you will have two waffles instead of one, half clinging to each side of the iron. If the waffle is a rather speckled brown, the iron is a bit too hot.

Use sour milk if you want good waffles. Buttermilk and sweet milk may be used (omit the soda and use three teaspoonfuls of baking powder with the latter), but they are not so good. You simply cannot get a crispy, tender waffle with anything but good, thick, sour milk.

SPANISH BUNS

1 pint flour	1 tablespoon cinnamon
1 pint sugar	1 teaspoon cloves
1 cup sweet milk	3 teaspoons baking powder
1 cup butter	
4 eggs, yolks and whites beaten separately	

Cream butter, add sugar, flavoring, milk, eggs, flour alternately. Roll out on a floured board and cut with a large glass or cup about an inch thick and bake in a moderate oven. When taken from oven sprinkle with sugar while hot.

SOFT CORN BREAD

3 eggs, beaten together	1 pinch salt
1 quart sweet milk	1 tablespoon melted lard
1 level teaspoon baking powder	Native yellow corn-meal

Use native yellow corn-meal to make a thin batter. Mix in order given. Put in baking dish and bake in a moderate oven. To keep eggs from forming on top, stir it up after five minutes in the oven. Serve from same dish, by a spoon.

SIPPETS

(To Serve with Fried Chicken)

One pint of corn-meal, one tablespoonful of lard, and enough water to make a mush. Make in small round cakes, and fry in hot lard. After frying the chickens, before making the gravy, fry the cakes in the same lard in which the chickens were cooked.

BARCELONA BUNS

(Angelica Muñoz)

1 quart milk	1 nutmeg, grated
1 pound butter	Little cinnamon
1 pound sugar	Flour
6 egg-yolks	1 gill yeast
1 wineglass brandy and rosewater	

To one pint milk add butter, sugar, brandy and rosewater, nutmeg, cinnamon, and egg-yolks. Stir in flour gradually until you can hardly stir it longer with a spoon. Then put in a gill of yeast in a pint of milk and set it to rise. A half pound of raisins cut fine can be added when you cut it down and knead it. Let it rise again, form into buns and bake.

PAN DE MALLORCA
(FRANCES DEL TORO)

8 ounces bread sponge	1 cup luke-warm water
12 tablespoons sugar	1 cup olive oil
6 well-beaten eggs	Butter
Flour	

To the bread sponge, sugar, well-beaten eggs and water, add enough flour to make a thin batter (about 10 A. M.). Let rise five hours, then add olive oil, 6 tablespoonfuls sugar, enough flour to knead. After kneading let it rise again till double its bulk which will be about 8 P. M. Divide in small pieces, grease lightly with butter, roll up, twist around in a circle like a tea-ring, place in a greased pan. Cover with a blanket and let rise until morning, when it should be baked in a moderately hot oven. This makes sixteen rolls.

DESERTS

"Behind Him lay the gay Azores,
Behind the gates of Hercules,
Behind him not the ghost of shores,
Before him only shoreless seas.
The good mate said, 'Now we must pray,
For, lo, the very stars are gone;
Speak, Admiral, now what shall I say?'
'Why, say, Sail on, sail on and on.' "

—*"Columbus", by Joaquin Miller.*

Is a sugar a fruit or a vegetable? Did you ever, when a child, pull a piece of blossoming grass and chewing on it, find it sweet to the taste? Well, believe it or not, sugar is a giant grass! Its long, succulent hard stems of varying colors are packed with wonderful juice which, boiled down, becomes converted into crystals called sugar. Sugar-cane is botanically known as *saccharum officinarum*.

The Arabs carried sugar into Egypt and the south of Spain, whence it was brought to the West Indies by early Spanish explorers. Columbus had carried plantings on his second voyage for Santo Domingo from where it, no doubt, was taken to other islands. The whole story of growing sugar, the development of cane breeding and chemistry, with tremendous influence on economics as well as social and cultural structure in countries where it is grown, provides material for an epic. In Puerto Rico, we trace it from humble, small beginnings to the romance of grinding fortunes from its luscious stalks, and now a great national industry, giving work to thousands of people.

It is said the first sugar planted in Puerto Rico for commercial purposes was in Isabela. Don Diego Lorenzo, Canonigo de Cabo Rojo, showed the Puerto Ricans how to make a mill to grind sugar in the sixteenth century.

It was not until the eighteenth century that any refinement of the old-fashioned brown sugar took place. Nothing can be compared with the luscious soft brown Muscovado sugar. It is so rich in syrup it leaves a lining on the sugar bowl; full of mineral salts and redolent in flavor, it had its place in our grandmother's pantries long after the white refined sugar was obtainable. The old-fashioned brown sugar is a real health food and gives a texture and flavor in baking that can be replaced by no other sugar.

CUSTARDS

Puerto Rican women excel in the making of custards, the recipes of which have come down in some families for generations. In order to insure success in the making of custards, great care should be exercised in having all the ingredients in a fresh state. In the baking of custards a moderate heat should only be used, and the dish should be well buttered.

It is best to place the custard in an earthen dish and set this in a vessel partly filled with hot water in a moderate oven until done. A dripping pan containing hot water will answer.

It is best to mix a level tablespoonful of sifted flour with the sugar first, before putting in the other ingredients.

Three or four eggs to each pint of milk is the general rule. In case you desire the custard very rich, cream should be used instead of milk, and more eggs must be used. A small lump of butter can also be added.

In adding beaten eggs to hot milk, add a little cold milk to the eggs first and then stir this into the hot milk a little at a time, stirring constantly.

The yolks of the eggs should be first beaten separately, then the sugar should be added, and this again beaten well. Then add the beaten whites of the eggs and the flavoring, and add all a little at a time into the milk, stirring constantly.

If you desire to impart a nice flavor to the custards and meringues, beat a little fruit jelly with the white of the eggs. Vanilla, lemon, almond or any other flavor may also be used in making custards.

CUSTARD

4 eggs
1 pint rich new milk
1 ounce sugar or more

6 young laurel leaves
or grated lemon peel

Use about four eggs to a pint of rich new milk. Flavor the milk by putting six young laurel leaves or grated lemon peel into it, before beginning to make the custard, and leaving them until it is done; sweeten the milk with an ounce or more of sugar, according to taste. Beat up the eggs thoroughly with sugar and add the milk to it boiling hot. Place all in the saucepan and stir it over a slow fire until it begins to thickens. Then remove it from the fire and continue stirring it until it is of exactly the right thickness. Turn it out immediately and keep stirring it until it is cool.

CUP CUSTARD

4 eggs
1 small half cup sugar
Flavoring

1 quart milk
2 even tablespoons cornstarch

Heat the milk to a boiling point and stir in the cornstarch dissolved in a little cold water; then add the yolks and sugar beaten together. Fill the cups two-thirds full of the custard. Pile on top of them the whites, beaten to a stiff froth with about a tablespoon of sugar, then bake to a light brown.

FLOATING ISLAND

4 cups fresh milk
5 ounces sugar
5 eggs

Flavoring
3 tablespoons currant jelly
3 tablespoons sugar for meringue

Heat the milk, then add the beaten yolks and one of the whites, together with the sugar. First stir into them a little of the milk to prevent curdling, then all of the milk. Do not have the milk boiling. Cook it the proper thickness, remove from the fire, and when cool, flavor; then pour it into a glass dish and let it become very cold. Before it is served, beat up the remaining three egg-whites to a stiff froth, and beat into them three tablespoonfuls of sugar and two tablespoonfuls of currant jelly. Dip this over the top of the custard.

LEMON CUSTARD

4 eggs
1 lemon

Sugar
Madeira wine or brandy

Beat the yolks of four eggs till they are white, pour on them one-half pint of boiling water, add the juice and grated rind of one lemon, sweeten to taste, then add one-half glass of Madeira wine or a fourth glass of brandy. Then scald it over the fire until it thickens. When cool put in glass cups. To be eaten cold.

PISTACHIO CUSTARD

1 pint milk
2 or 3 eggs
½ cup sugar

1½ ounce pistachio nuts
Spinach juice

Add a pint of milk to two or three well-beaten eggs, sweeten with a scant half cup of sugar, and stir into this one ounce and one-half of pistachio nuts, previously scalded, the skins rubbed off, and ground very fine in the nut-grinder. Cook the whole as for a soft custard, and when thick add a few drops of spinach juice or green vegetable coloring matter until the mixture is delicately tinted green.

ST. THOMAS TRIFLE

Bake a sponge cake quite flat, saturate with peach brandy or any cordial. Just before sending to the table cover it with whipped cream sweetened with sugar and wine.

FRUIT CREAM

4 bananas
2 oranges
1 tablespoon lemon juice
1 tablespoon sherry wine

⅔ cup powdered sugar
1¼ tablespoons gelatine
1 cup whipped cream

Peel and mash four bananas, rub through a sieve. Add pulp and juice of two oranges, one tablespoon lemon juice, one tablespoon sherry wine, two-thirds cup powdered sugar and one and one-fourth tablespoons gelatine dissolved in one-fourth cup boiling water. Cool in ice water, stirring all the time, and fold it in a cup of whipped cream.

GYPSIES ARM

½ cup sugar
½ cup flour
3 eggs
2 teaspoonfuls milk

¼ teaspoon soda
½ teaspoon cream of tartar
¼ teaspoon salt

Beat egg-yolks and whites separately. When the yolks are well-beaten add the sifted sugar. Then add part of the egg-whites alternating with the flour which had added to it the soda, cream of tartar, and rind of lemon, until both are used.

Pour into a flat pan as for jelly roll and bake in a moderate oven, about 375°. Sprinkle with cinnamon and cool. While this bakes prepare the filling as follows:

SPANISH CREAM FILLING

1 cup milk	½ teaspoon salt
1 stick cinnamon	1 tablespoon butter
Piece lemon rind	4 egg-yolks
¾ cup sugar	Powdered sugar
¼ cup flour	

Bring to a boil the milk, cinnamon, lemon rind, and strain. Mix sugar, flour and salt and add slowly to the milk, cooking in a double-boiler fifteen minutes. Then add a tablespoon of butter and the beaten yolks of the eggs. Cook about three more minutes.

Spread this on the flat cake and roll as for a jelly roll. Dust with powdered sugar.

HONEY RECIPES

"Like the bee, culling honey from every flower, the virtuous sweets."—As You Like It.

THERE is perhaps no article of food more often referred to in ancient writings than honey.

Moses' song praised the Lord saying: "So the Lord alone did lead him. He made him ride on the high places of the earth that he might eat the increase of the fields, and he made him to suck honey out of the rock," and he spoke of bringing the children of Israel out of Egypt "into a land flowing with milk and honey." Isaiah said: "Butter and honey shall he eat that he may know to refuse the evil and to choose the good."

It was said in olden times where much honey was, there was much wool, the connection being that a tilled country would naturally produce flowers in abundance for the bees to sip from. Pliny and Xenophon both wrote of honey; it is mentioned in ancient Persian poetry; the Koran has a chapter devoted to bees; "there proceedeth from their bellies a licquor of various color wherein is a medicine for men." In Russia a delicious drink was made of honey from the lindens. Chaucer wrote of clare, a drink of wine, honey and spices.

Before cane sugar was introduced from the tropics, honey was the most used sweet. Wild honey is still gathered in many parts of the world. Honey is high in food value and is especially recommended for children as in addition to other mineral salts it contains much lime. An ordinary tablespoon of honey contains 100 calories. It is digested more quickly than cane sugar and is somewhat laxative. In olden times honey was very much used in the preparation of medicines providing an agreeable vehicle for strong herbs, if not for its own virtues.

Honey should be kept in a dry, warm place, not in an ice-box. It can be used in such a variety of ways it deserves wider attention than it normally receives in the diet. Many persons who are denied the use of cane sugar can readily bear the use of honey. It can be used in drinks and in almost any recipe calling for sweetening. Use it measure for measure in place of molasses; for sugar, a cupful will take the place of a cupful of sugar, only as the honey has about one-fifth of a cupful of water in it, allowance should be made in measuring, for this moisture.

In cook books of the olden times spices are used which seem unusual, but experience doubtless has shown that it is a good combination. For example, in Spanish cookery there is a good deal of anise and cardamon. Cardamon seeds have been used much more in Europe than in American cookery.

Coriander seeds are also used, and a government bulletin, compiled after comparing cookbooks of various countries, gives the following combination of spices to mix and keep on hand to use with honey:

2 ounces ground cinnamon	½ ounce ground cloves
1 ounce ground coriander seed	2 ounces anise seed

Another mixture is made of:

Salt, 1 part	Ginger, 4 parts
White pepper, 1 part	Cardamon seeds, 8 parts
Nutmeg, 2 parts	Cinnamon, 16 parts
Cloves, 2 parts	

The flavor of honey, of course, depends upon the flowers from which the bees derive the nectar. In the north we hear of buckwheat honey and its richness, and the clarity of clover honey; but bees in Puerto Rico live in a veritable paradise, since there is such an embarrassments of riches. All the lovely fragrant vines, the garden flowers that are rich in nectar, to say nothing of the coffee trees and fruit trees, of which some are in flower the year round, so that there is always nectar for the busy bee, and the resulting honey is delicious.

BRAN BROWN BREAD

1 cup white or whole wheat flour	½ cup honey
1 teaspoon soda	1 cup sour milk
¼ teaspoon salt	½ cup raisins, floured
1 cup bran	

Sift together the flour, soda, and salt, and add the other ingredients.

Steam three hours or bake 40 minutes in a slow oven. If the amount of milk is increased by half, the bread is more delicate and has a somewhat higher food value.

STEAMED BROWN BREAD

1 cup yellow corn-meal	1 teaspoon salt
2 cups graham flour	1½ teaspoons soda
⅔ cup honey	1 tablespoon boiling water
2 cups sour milk	1 cup seeded raisins

Mix together the meal, flour, and salt; add the sour milk and the honey and then the soda dissolved in the boiling water; and the raisins. Steam three hours in covered receptacles, which should be not more than two-thirds full at the beginning of the cooking.

HONEY BREAD

2 cups honey	4 teaspoons powdered cardamon seed
4 cups rye flour	2 egg-yolks
1 teaspoon soda	¼ cup brown sugar
4 teaspoons anise seed	2 teaspoons ginger

Sift the flour with the spices and soda and add the other ingredients. Put the dough into shallow buttered pans to the depth of about an inch and bake in a hot oven.

HONEY AND NUT BRAN MUFFINS

½ cup honey	1 tablespoon melted butter
1 cup flour	1½ cups milk
¼ to ½ teaspoon soda	¾ cup finely chopped English walnuts
2 cups bran	

Sift together the flour, soda, and salt, and mix them with the bran. Add the other ingredients and bake for 25 or 30 minutes in a hot oven in gem tins. This will make about sixteen large muffins, each of which may be considered roughly as a 100-calories portion and to contain 2 grams of protein.

HARD HONEY CAKE

¾ cup honey	½ teaspoon cloves
½ cup sugar	Speck white pepper
2½ cups flour	Speck salt
1 egg	½ teaspoon soda
¼ teaspoon ginger	1 tablespoon water
1 teaspoon cinnamon	2 ounces blanched almonds cut into
½ teaspoon ground cardamon seed	small pieces or chopped

Sift together the flour and spices, dissolve the soda in the water, beat the egg and combine all the ingredients. Beat or knead the mixture thoroughly. Cook a small sample. If it does not rise sufficiently, add a little more soda and honey; if it falls, add a little more flour. Roll out the dough to the thickness of about three-fourths of an inch and bake in a hot oven. When the cake is done glaze it with a thick syrup of sugar and water and allow it to dry in a slow oven or in some other warm place. While it is still warm, cut it into long strips. Or it may be left in one large cake, to be cut into very thin slices when served. This cake will become very hard on cooling and will not be soft enough to eat for several weeks, but will keep in good condition for an indefinite length of time.

BUTTER HONEY CAKE

1½ cups honey
½ cup butter
3 egg yolks
5 cups flour
2 teaspoons ground cinnamon

½ teaspoon salt
1½ teaspoons soda
2 tablespoons orange-flower water.
 (Water may be substituted)
3 egg-whites

Rub together the honey and butter; add the unbeaten yolks and beat thoroughly. Add the flour sifted with the cinnamon and the salt; add the soda dissolved in the orange-flower water. Beat the mixture thoroughly and add the well-beaten whites of the eggs. Bake in shallow tins and cover with frosting made as follows:

ORANGE FROSTING FOR BUTTER HONEY CAKE

Grated rind 1 orange
1 teaspoon lemon juice

1 tablespoon orange juice
1 egg yolk

Confectioners' sugar

Mix all ingredients but the sugar and allow the mixture to stand for an hour. Strain and add confectioners' sugar until the frosting is sufficiently thick to be spread on the cake.

NUT HONEY CAKE

2 cups brown sugar
2 cups honey
6 egg-yolks
3 cups flour
Speck of salt
1½ teaspoons soda
3 teaspoons ground cinnamon
½ teaspoon ground cloves

Whites of 3 eggs
½ teaspoon ground nutmeg
½ teaspoon allspice
1 cup chopped raisins
½ ounce citron cut in small pieces
½ ounce candied orange peel cut
 in small pieces
½ pound almonds coarsely chopped

Mix the sugar, honey, and the yolks of the eggs, and beat thoroughly. Sift together the flour, salt, spices, and soda. Combine all ingredients but the whites of the eggs. Beat the whites of the eggs till they are stiff and add them last. Pour the dough to the depth of about half an inch well-buttered tins, and bake in a slow oven for one-half hour.

Frosting for Nut Honey Cake

1½ cups sugar   3 egg-whites   ¾ cup water

Boil the sugar and water until the syrup forms a thread when dropped from the spoon. While still hot, pour the syrup over the well-beaten whites of eggs, beating the mixture until it is of the right consistency to spread.

CHOCOLATE NUT HONEY CAKE

To the above add 3 ounces of chocolate grated.

SOFT HONEY CAKE

½ cup butter   1 teaspoon soda
1 cup honey   ½ teaspoon cinnamon
1 egg   ½ teaspoon ginger
½ cup sour milk   4 cups flour

Rub the butter and honey together; add the egg well-beaten, then the sour milk and the flour sifted with the soda and spices. Bake in a shallow pan.

HONEY SPONGE CAKE

½ cup sugar   4 eggs
½ cup honey   1 cup sifted flour

Mix the sugar and honey and boil until the syrup will spin a thread when dropped from the spoon. Pour the syrup over the yolks of the eggs which have been beaten until light. Beat this mixture until cold; then add the flour, and cut and fold the beaten whites of the eggs into the mixture. Bake for 40 or 50 minutes in a pan lined with buttered paper, in a slow oven.

This cake can be made with a cupful of unheated honey in place of the honey and sugar syrup, but the quality is not quite so good.

HONEY POUND CAKE

A good pound cake can be made by using equal weights of honey, sugar, eggs, flour, and butter. A little soda should be added because of the acidity of the honey, and a good flavoring is cardamon seed and orange-flower water. Or a cake similar to pound cake may be made as follows:

1 cup sugar   2 cups pastry flour
¾ cup honey   ½ teaspoon powdered cardamon seeds
1 cup butter   ½ teaspoon soda
4 eggs   ½ teaspoon orange-flower water

Rub together the butter and sugar, and add the honey. Add the yolks of the eggs well-beaten. Finally, add the whites of the eggs, beaten to a stiff froth, and the orange-flower water. Add gradually the flour sifted with the soda and cardamon seed. Beat the mixture for ten minutes. Put the dough into a warm tin with high sides, and bake in a slow oven one hour.

HONEY FRUIT CAKE

3 cups flour
2 teaspoons soda
3½ cups honey
1 cup butter
6 eggs
2 teaspoons cinnamon
2 teaspoons ginger
3 teaspoons ground cardamon seed
½ teaspoon cloves
3 pounds raisins (seeded)

1½ pounds currants
1 pound citron
1 pound candied cherries
1 pound candied apricots
1 pound candied pineapple
½ cup sour jelly, or
    ½ cup white grape juice
2 teaspoons vanilla
2 ounces candied orange peel
2 ounces candied lemon peel

Cut the candied fruit into small pieces, with the exception of the cherries which should be left whole. Place the fruit in a large dish and sift over it one-half of the flour, mixing thoroughly. Sift the soda with the remainder of the flour. Bring the honey and the butter to boiling point and while still hot add the spices. When the mixture is cool, add the well-beaten yolks of the eggs, then the flour and grape juice or jelly and the well-beaten whites. Finally, add the fruit. The cake should be divided into three or four parts and put into buttered dishes covered with buttered paper tied closely over the tops. Steam for five hours, remove the paper, and bake in a very slow oven for an hour. This makes a very rich cake consisting chiefly of fruit. For the sake of economy, the flour can be increased to even twice the quantity without affecting the quality very much.

CHRISTMAS CAKE

¾ cup honey
½ cup sugar
2 cups or more flour
½ teaspoon powdered ginger
½ teaspoon cardamon seed ground to a powder
⅛ teaspoon cloves

Speck white pepper
Pinch salt
¼ to ½ teaspoon soda
1 tablespoon water
2 ounces blanched almonds
    chopped fine

Cream the butter, sugar and honey and slowly add the dry ingredients, the water last of all. Bake as for fruit cake.

YELLOW HONEY CAKE

½ cup sugar
2 egg-yolks
⅔ cup honey

¼ teaspoon cinnamon
⅛ teaspoon cloves
1½ cups flour

Sift together the flour and the spices. Mix the sugar and egg-yolks, add the honey, and then the flour gradually. Roll out thin, moisten the surface with egg-white, and mark into small squares. Bake in a moderate oven.

HONEY COOKIES

⅔ cup honey	1 teaspoon cloves
⅔ cup sugar	1 teaspoon allspice
2½ cups flour	2 ounces finely chopped candied orange peel
½ teaspoon soda	¼ pound walnut meats finely chopped
1½ teaspoons cinnamon	

Sift together the flour, spices, and soda, and add the other ingredients. Knead thoroughly, roll out thin, and cut with a biscuit-cutter. These cookies are very hard.

HONEY BRAN COOKIES

2 tablespoons butter	½ cup flour
½ cup honey	1 cup bran
2 eggs	⅛ teaspoon powdered anise seed
¼ to ½ teaspoon soda	

Rub together the butter and honey; add the eggs unbeaten, and beat the mixture thoroughly. Sift together the flour, soda, and anise seed. Combine all the ingredients; drop from a teaspoon on a buttered tin and bake in a moderate oven.

BAKED HONEY CUSTARD

5 eggs	⅛ teaspoon powdered cinnamon
½ cup honey	½ teaspoon salt
4 cups scalded milk	

Beat the eggs sufficiently to unite the yolks and whites, but not enough to make them foamy. Add the other ingredients and bake in cups or in a large pan in a moderate oven. The baking dishes should be set in water.

BOILED HONEY CUSTARD

2 cups milk	⅓ cup honey
3 egg yolks	⅛ teaspoon salt

Mix the honey, eggs, and salt. Scald the milk and pour it over the eggs. Cook in a double-boiler until the mixture thickens. This custard is suitable for use in place of cream on gelatine desserts, or to be poured over sliced oranges or stewed fruit.

HONEY PUDDING

½ cup honey	½ teaspoon ginger
6 ounces bread-crumbs	2 egg-yolks
½ cup milk	2 tablespoons butter
Rind of ½ lemon	2 egg-whites

Mix the honey and the bread-crumbs and add the milk, seasoning, and yolks of the eggs. Beat the mixture thoroughly and then add the butter and the whites of the eggs well-beaten. Steam for about two hours in a pudding mould which is not more than three-quarters full.

HONEY CHARLOTTE RUSSE

1 quart cream   6 lady fingers   ½ cup delicately flavored honey

Chill the honey by placing the dish containing it in a pan of ice-water. Whip the cream and add it to the honey, mixing the two well. Line a dish with lady fingers and fill it with the honey and cream. Serve very cold.

HONEY MOUSSE

4 eggs   1 pint cream   1 cup hot, delicately flavored honey

Beat the eggs slightly and slowly pour over them the hot honey. Cook until the mixture thickens. When it is cool, add the cream whipped. Put the mixture into a mold, pack in salt and ice, and let stand three or four hours.

HONEY ICE CREAM No. 1

1 quart thin cream   ¾ cup delicately flavored honey

Mix ingredients and freeze.

HONEY ICE CREAM No. 2

1 pint milk   1 cup honey
6 egg-yolks   1 pint cream

Heat the milk in a double boiler. Beat together the honey and eggs, add the hot milk, return the mixture to the double-boiler, and cook it until it thickens. Add the cream and when the mixture is cool, freeze it.

ROSELLE PRESERVES

A very good preserve may be made from roselle petals and honey which will remain in good condition for a long time. Take equal weights of roselle petals, honey, and water. Cook the petals in the honey and water until soft. Remove and boil down the syrup until just enough remains to cover. Pour into glasses and cover as you would jelly.

SAUCE FOR ICE CREAM

2 tablespoons butter   2 teaspoons cornstarch   ½ cup honey

Cook together the cornstarch and butter thoroughly, being careful not to brown them. Add the honey and cook the mixture until it becomes hard when dropped into cold water and until all taste of raw cornstarch has been removed.

SALAD DRESSING

4 egg-yolks	1 teaspoon mustard
2 tablespoons vinegar or lemon juice	1 teaspoon salt
2 tablespoons butter	Paprika to taste
2 tablespoons honey	1 cup cream

Heat the cream in a double boiler. Beat the eggs, and add to them all the other ingredients but the cream. Pour the cream slowly over the mixture, beating constantly. Pour it into the double-boiler and cook until it thickens, or mix all the ingredients but the cream and cook in a double-boiler until the mixture thickens. As the dressing is needed combine this mixture with whipped cream. This dressing is particularly suitable for fruit salads.

NOUGAT

3/8 cup honey	1 pound almonds
1/2 cup brown sugar	2 egg-whites

Boil the honey and sugar together until drops of the mixture hold their shape when poured into cold water. Add the whites of the eggs, well-beaten, and cook very slowly, stirring constantly, until the mixture becomes brittle when dropped into water. Add the almonds and cool under a weight. The candy can be broken into pieces, or may be cut and wrapped in waxed-paper.

HONEY FUDGE

2 cups sugar	1/3 cup water
1/3 cup honey	2 egg-whites
1 teaspoon of vanilla extract	

Boil together the sugar, honey, and water until the syrup spins a thread when dropped from the spoon (about 250° F.). Pour the syrup over the well-beaten whites of the eggs, beating continuously and until the mixture crystallizes, adding the flavoring after the mixture has cooled a little. Drop in small pieces on buttered or paraffin paper. The vanilla may be omitted.

HONEY CARAMELS

2 cups granulated sugar	1/4 cup honey
1/2 cup cream or milk	1/4 cup butter

Mix the ingredients; heat and stir until the sugar is dissolved; then cook without stirring until a firm ball can be formed from a little of the mixture dropped into cold water. Beat the mixture until it crystallizes, pour into buttered pans, and cut into squares. The addition of pecan nuts improves these caramels.

Sugar can be omitted and honey substituted in its place in almost any of these recipes.

In Puerto Rico the country people make long candles of beeswax. They are sold in the country shops tied together in bunches.

CHRISTMAS DISHES

"Strong hands to weak, old hands to young, around the Christmas board, touch hands."—John Norton's "Vagabond."

AT Christmas time groups of singers or players go from house to house singing carols, *villancicos* or *aguinaldos,* many of which have come down to us from long, long ago. It is the custom to give the performers some small gift or refreshment. Often it is *pasteles* for there is sure to be a supply on hand for the holidays, for festivals have their traditional dishes. In Puerto Rico as in other Spanish-speaking countries, Christmas Eve is *Noche Buena,* when there are serenades and supper parties before the *Misa de Gallo,* Midnight Mass. The real day of gifts is Three Kings Day, the sixth of January, Twelfth Night or Little Christmas in northern countries; it is Epiphany in the Church calendar. On the evening of the fifth night little children are to be seen filling boxes with grass; these they put under their beds when they go to bed and during the night the Three Kings pass by, refresh their horses with the grass and leave toys and gifts in its place.

A popular *aguinaldo* sung at that time is the following:

"Si me dan pasteles   If you give me pasteles
 Demelos caliente   Give them to me hot
I Que pasteles frios   For cold pasteles
 Empachan la gente."   Surfeit the people.

The word *aguinaldo* means Christmas gift or New Year's gift.

PASTELES
(America Gaztambide)

FILLING:

½ pound beef
½ pound pork
Small piece ham
½ cup shelled almonds
1 cup raisins
¼ cup cut-up olives

1 tablespoon capers
1 tablespoon minced sweet pepper
1 teaspoon salt
Few drops Tabasco sauce
1 tablespoon butter or lard

OUTSIDE WRAPPING:

6 mafafo plantains
Yellow yautias
1 egg
1 tablespoon lard

Salt and pepper
Milk
Plantain leaves

Prepare a filling by chopping the meats (grinding makes them too fine) and adding almonds, raisins, olives, capers, salt, sweet pepper, butter or lard and a few drops of Tabasco sauce. Some like to cook this together but it has a better flavor if left raw. Mix and set aside until outside part is prepared.

Now grate six "mafafo" plantains (very green) and a few yellow yautias; there should be half as much grated yautia as plantain. The yautia makes it nice and smooth. Mix it together with an egg, salt and pepper, a spoon of lard and enough milk to spread. Take nicely washed plantain leaves cut in squares; these come prepared in the market. Spread with a little lard or butter, then the plantain paste, and then a large spoonful of the meat allowing enough of the paste to turn over the meat like a turnover, fold over the leaf and turn down the ends. Tie it both ways around so that no water will enter and plunge it into boiling water to cook an hour. Pasteles may be made in advance and kept in the ice-box, reheated when wanted. Do not remove from the leaf until ready to serve and always send them piping hot to the table.

PASTELES DE ARROZ

Boil and mash the rice and use it instead of plantain or yautia to envelop the meat filling.

One may also use yuca or apio. Wash and peel the root, grate it and put in a piece of cheesecloth to express all the water. Take the dry grated root then to make the paste for the pasteles.

HALLACAS
FILLING:

Equal parts pork and beef
Bacon
1 cup bread-crumbs
½ cup almonds

Raisins
1 tablespoon capers
1 tablespoon lard
Salt and pepper

WRAPPING:

Corn-meal	Salt
Milk	Plantain leaves

Prepare the meat filling by grinding meats and a bit of bacon; add bread-crumbs, almonds, raisins, capers, lard, salt and pepper to taste and mix well. Cook slightly.

Make a mush of corn-meal, add salt, enough milk to make it a consistency to spread and proceed as for pasteles. Mexican tamales are made in the same way, but are seasoned more highly and corn husks are used in place of plantain leaves.

HALLACAS—No. 2

(CONCHITA TORRES)

1 pound white corn-meal	1 can Spanish sweet peppers
½ pound beef	Capers
½ pound pork	Few strips bacon
1 chicken	½ box seedless raisins
½ pound lard with achiote	1 small bottle sour pickle
1 bottle olives	

Cook the corn-meal the day before. On the following day strain off any water it may have, add the lard little by little, cover with a cloth. Cut the meat very fine and cook it. Cook the bacon and cut into small pieces. Cut the sweet peppers. Lay on a platter the egg, almonds, pickle, raisins, capers, olives. Take large plantain leaves and small ones cut perfectly square. With a spatula take the corn-meal, put some on a large leaf four inches square and spread it very thin to that size, then do the same on a small leaf spreading it thin as possible. Then upon the part that is on the large leaf put a spoonful of meat, two or three capers, an almond, bacon, pepper, a slice of egg, a piece of pickle. Upon this place the small leaf squaring so that the corn-meal joins, and it forms a perfect square. Wrap this in a still larger leaf keeping it all square. Tie with four threads around it. Put water on to boil and salt it. When boiling put in the hallacas and let them boil an hour. Take out and set to drain. Making this dish one day and reheating it in the broiler, makes it very tasty.

MANJAR BLANCO

1 cup rice flour	1 tablespoon orange-flower water
2½ cups milk	1½ cups sugar
1 tablespoon lard	

Cook slowly stirring constantly until done and then pour it into a shallow platter which has been greased so it will not stick.

MAJARETTE (Corn-meal Pudding)
(Sarah Mendez)

2 cups corn-meal	1 tablespoon butter
1 tablespoon flour	2 eggs
½ cup sugar	1 teaspoon salt
1 cup milk	

Bring corn-meal, flour, sugar, and milk, to boil with a tablespoon butter. When it begins to boil add two beaten egg-yolks and a teaspoon salt. Take from the fire, add the beaten whites of the eggs and put in a pudding dish and bake in a moderate oven. Serve hot.

ALMOJABANAS
(Elsie Domenech)

2 cups rice flour	12 eggs
1 cup grated native cheese	1½ teaspoon salt
1 tablespoon butter	Fat for frying
¼ cup hot milk	

Put the cheese in a bowl and add the milk and salt. Add the flour a little at a time, then the butter and the eggs Drop by spoonfuls into hot deep fat and fry a golden brown.

PUERTO RICO PUDDING

3 cups milk	2 cups sugar
3 beaten eggs	1 tablespoon cinnamon
3 cups dry, rolled bread-crumbs	1 teaspoon cloves
3 dessertspoons melted butter	1 cup toasted almonds, cut fine
1 cup raisins soaked in dry wine	

Add well-beaten eggs to the milk, then bread-crumbs, butter, sugar, spices, almonds, and raisins that have been previously soaked in dry wine. Mix well and put in well-buttered ramekins. Set them in a pan of water and bake in a moderate oven until nicely browned.

SWEET RICE

1 pound rice	1 tablespoon cassava
7 cups water	1 teaspoon salt
1 cup sugar	1 tablespoon anise seed pounded in a mortar
1 small hand ginger	1 tablespoon cinnamon
Tiny bits of cloves	4 tablespoons lard

Add the salt and sugar to the water and put on to boil. When it reaches boiling add the rice. Pound the ginger and strain adding a bit of water. Stir the rice if necessary with a fork. When it begins to dry add the lard and stir, gradually adding the spices. Keep on a slow fire until the grains of rice are done and dry. Then when serving add the cassava.

CREOLE CASSEROLE

Milk of 1 coconut	2 pounds sweet potato
2 pounds yautia	4 pounds squash
1 pound rice flour	3 pounds sugar
5 eggs	1 glass wine
½ pint cow's milk	Cloves and cinnamon

Boil and mash the vegetables, strain, add coconut milk, two eggs without beating, sugar, cloves, cinnamon, the wine and the flour. Add sufficient cow's milk to give a good consistency. Add the other three eggs, put in a greased mould and bake in a moderate oven, trying it with a clean straw from time to time.

GANDINGA

Take pigs' liver and cut it up. Add crushed pepper, salt, parsley or culantro. Brown in lard colored with achiote, add water to cover and let it stew. Thicken the broth and serve with boiled rice.

EMPANADILLAS

(SRTA. CABANILLAS)

1½ cups flour	1 egg-white
½ teaspoon salt	2 egg-yolks
¼ pound butter	

Make a pastry with above ingredients, adding all to flour with just enough water to roll onto the pastry board. Cut in rounds the size of a small plate. Onto a round put a large spoonful of the following filling, cover with another round, pinch the edges together like you would pie, and bake in the oven.

FILLING

3 tablespoons lard	1 tablespoon olives cut up
3 tablespoons minced onions	1 tablespoon capers
¼ cup tomato sauce	1 tablespoon raisins
1 cup ground pork meat	¼ spoon cayenne pepper
1 teaspoon salt	

Cook the filling fifteen minutes. Hard-boiled eggs are sometimes added. The mixture may be varied to suit one's taste. These may also be made by cutting the pastry into squares, doubling over half so that the empanadillas are triangular in shape, and drop them into hot lard to cook.

Very tiny empanadillas cut the size of a small cookie are good to serve with cocktails.

RUM OMELETTE

(Santos Felipe)

6 eggs
6 tablespoons cold water
3 tablespoons butter
1 cup fruit cut fine

1 teaspoon salt
1 tablespoon brown sugar
1 teaspoon powdered sugar

Beat the eggs together with the water, salt and sugar. Melt the butter in an omelette pan, add the eggs. When they begin to set, lift "poco a poco" (little by little) with a flat knife to let the fluid on top run under the cooked part, lay fruit over top and fold over. (Take it up before it cooks entirely for the rum burning will finish cooking the eggs.) When eggs are set, lift onto a hot platter, sprinkle with powdered sugar, pour over one cup best rum and light it as you send it to the table. Let it burn until the flame exhausts itself.

INDEX

Vegetables:

ELIZA B. K. DOOLEY

Writer, musician, artist, social worker devoted mother, and collector and tester of recipes, Mrs. Henry W. (Eliza B. K.) Dooley has been and continues to be all of these. Besides, for more than seven years Mrs. Dooley has served as Commissioner of Immigration and Naturalization in Puerto Rico; and for some years she has conducted a real estate business left her by her husband. She still finds time to make a genuine home with all that that implies.

Coming to Puerto Rico more than forty years ago, Mrs. Dooley's first big task was to learn Spanish, as she did not want to speak the "kitchen" dialect that many Americans in Puerto Rico confuse with the language. This knowledge of true Spanish has always stood her in good stead as she is socially prominent and counts among her friends the first families of the Island.

Her interest in the natives and the native foods has always been active, and soon after coming to Puerto Rico she familiarized herself with both through friendly visits with the people in their simple homes.

The author is a fine musician and has appeared in concerts in the United States and Puerto Rico. She is also a gifted painter, but her hobby in art is silhouettes. She has illustrated her own book.

Mrs. Dooley always advocates: "Eat the foods of the country in which you live," and she tries to encourage this among Americans and others in Puerto Rico. Her extraordinary research in the fine foods of the Island led her to write this book.

COACHWHIP PUBLICATIONS
CoachwhipBooks.com

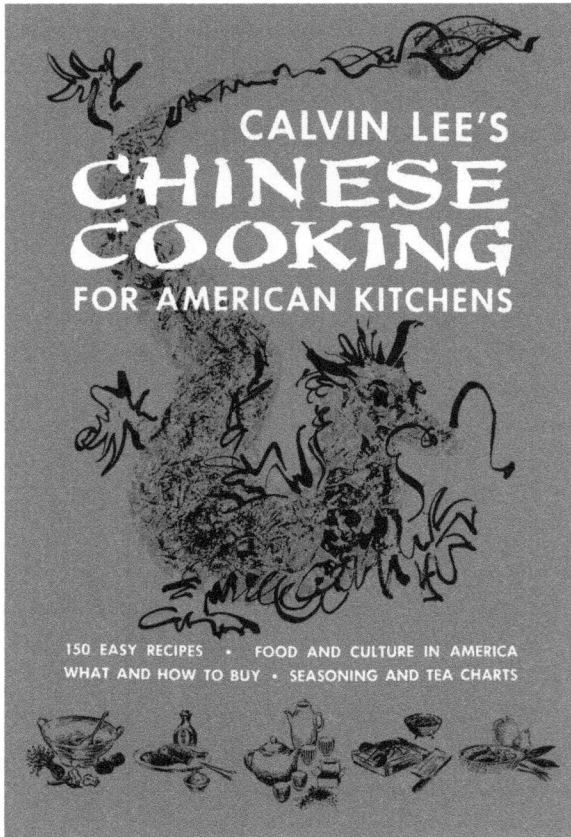

CALVIN LEE'S
CHINESE COOKING
FOR AMERICAN KITCHENS

150 EASY RECIPES · FOOD AND CULTURE IN AMERICA
WHAT AND HOW TO BUY · SEASONING AND TEA CHARTS

COACHWHIP PUBLICATIONS
CoachwhipBooks.com

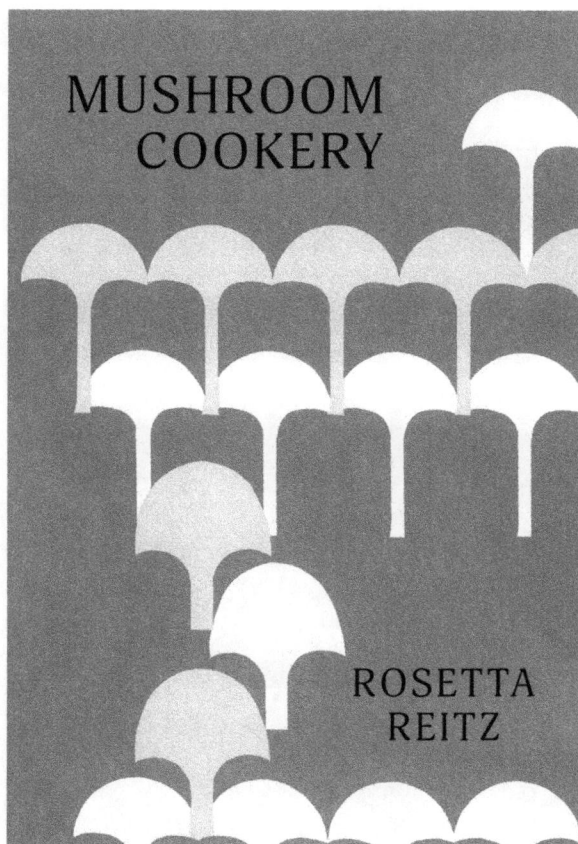

MUSHROOM COOKERY

ROSETTA REITZ

COACHWHIP PUBLICATIONS
CoachwhipBooks.com

SPAGHETTI
DINNER

BY
GIUSEPPE
PREZZOLINI

COACHWHIP PUBLICATIONS
CoachwhipBooks.com

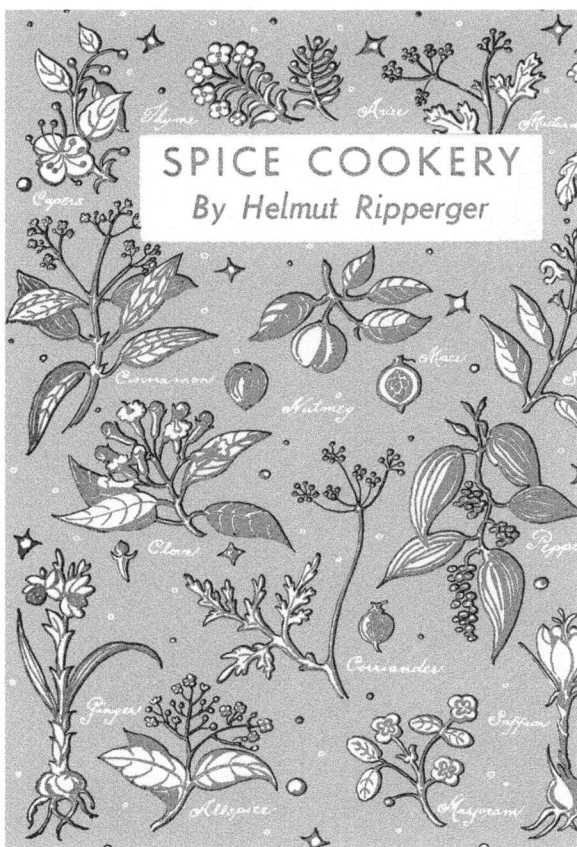

SPICE COOKERY
By Helmut Ripperger

www.ingramcontent.com/pod-product-compliance
Lightning Source LLC
Chambersburg PA
CBHW031132090426
42738CB00008B/1053